INCEST

The Curse of Destruction...Reversed

An Overcomer's Testimony

SANDRA CERDA

New Life Publishing

Bringing **1st Time Authors**, to *print!*

On Facebook@1stTimeAuthors

FOR THE CHILD IN EVERY ADULT
WHO CONTINUES TO CRY OUT TO GOD FOR
UNDERSTANDING, AND FREEDOM...

...AND FOR MY LOVED ONES WHO HAVE OVERCOME;
WHOSE OWN PURE LOVE AND FORGIVENESS
ENCOURAGED ME TO CONTINUE SEEKING ABSOLUTE
LIBERTY FROM THE *PAIN OF INCEST and RAPE.*

CONTENTS

A Letter from the Author

You may never understand. There may always be answers you may never receive, to questions you will always have. There may be missing pieces to the puzzle of life's despair and pain, that you *may not ever find.* If you will get the broken, wounded, and worn pieces that you do have and take them to Jesus Christ... you'll find all your answers in the Lord.

You will find in Him a peace of mind that passes all the understanding you are ever going to need. You will find that He has always been the missing piece of life and you will enter a place of wholeness, as Jesus begins a daily healing, a daily cleansing, a daily restoring of your hurt and shattered soul.

You will discover, He never intended for those moments of pain to ever happen to you, but He will help you work those past hurts into your life and overcome them in His strength.

As you continue your walk with Him, ever increasing in the firm reliance of His might, He will enable you to face those memories of torment and anguish; a day at a time, a step at a time.

He will give you the grace you need to pray for those who have hurt you, and in His mercy **you will triumph over** *your experience, as you are transformed from victim... to victor, in Christ Jesus.*

This book is written for individuals who have experienced the tearing away of one's innocence through incest; and for those whose loved ones have experienced this trauma, and need a clearer and greater understanding of the depth of this pain, and the One Way to absolute liberty. For where the Spirit of the Lord is there is liberty!

The entirety of this book is taken from my own personal experience as a victim of incest whose whole life pattern was one of destruction and defeat, until I opened the door of my heart to Jesus Christ and allowed Him to enter my life; areas of my life that no one else had ever known about. Secret places so dark and areas so very painful that it took the strength of the Almighty God Himself to wash the pain and remove the shame and guilt, completely.

It is dedicated to freedom, absolute and true freedom found only in a *personal relationship* with Jesus Christ and in the realm of His forgiveness.

Allow this book to serve as a tool in ministering hope, through the ultimate delivering power of God's forgiveness, as you seek the Lord and enter the realm of final and complete triumph over the pain and trauma of your spirit, soul and body.

God bless you on *this* journey...

Sandra Cerda

CHAPTER ONE

THE THIEF COMES TO STEAL, KILL AND DESTROY

YEAR 1967

*H*ondo, Texas wasn't much of a town at the time, but it was the place the Lord chose for me; *"God's Country"*, the billboard at the town's entrance, read:

"Please Don't Drive Thru It Like Hell"

The first of all grandchildren in my mother's family, I was showered with love and like *many little girls,* nicknamed Princess. I hold many fond memories of my childhood; and some that are *not so fond.*

In 1967, my daddy was twenty-two when he left my mother alone to care for me and my baby brother. He was leaving for Viet Nam. Stationed in Chu Lai with the Light Infantry Brigade, they were attached with the 33rd Ranger Force Division of South Viet Nam. On a search and destroy mission near the Long Binh area, a Viet Cong sniper shot him on the left side of his head, as his buddy yelled *"take cover"!* After sixteen days' unconscious, he awakened in the Long Binh hospital.

Transferred to the 249th General Hospital in Japan, he

remained several weeks where he died... *and was revived.* His complications included brain damage with total loss of hearing to his left ear, severe impairment to his left eye, complete paralysis to the left side of his entire body. The paralysis was also expected to affect the right side of his body, but did not. Miraculously, he was again walking by the time he reached his base in San Antonio, Texas a few months after his injury.

Disabled, he soon returned to his home-town of Hondo, Texas. Not long afterwards he and my mother divorced. It was about that time, near the age of four, my mother surrendered our care over to her mother and stepfather. She was young and for reasons I may never understand, *we were suddenly there.* In truth, I still struggle with mothers who do that with their children. I remember many, many times alone at night, crying for her; *and it would be a long time before I would see my daddy again.*

Although my father and mother forsake me, yet the Lord will take me up (adopt me as His child).
PSALM 27:10

My brother and I were cared for at a Christian daycare facility during working hours. *This was the first place I heard about Jesus.* I recall clearly the first day we stayed there, I cried as my step-grandfather left me. Running to him, I clung tightly to his leg, but he left me anyway. My grandmother was a nurses-aide and worked the 7am-3pm shift. Every day, as I heard the whistle blow from the Kerrville State Hospital, I knew she was on her way to me, no matter where I was. Some days, we would stay home with my step-grandpa.

I don't remember too clearly, exactly when it all started. I remember it was cold outside, and nighttime. Other times it was bright, with sunny afternoons. But he began to touch me, making me feel uncomfortable. He would want me to sit on his lap or knee and he would rub his body against me. It was not long before I tried to avoid him when he called. I recall one day a week he would stay home and before long he began keeping us with him on those days.

On one of those days, he introduced us to a game he called *"chase."* We ran as fast as we could, screaming, and afraid as he chased us through the three-bedroom house; knowing if he caught us we would have to do whatever he wanted.

Eventually he would corner us in a bedroom, backing us up against the headboard; crawling from the foot of the bed toward us, with a grin on his face and a glare in his eye I will never forget, he said he had won. He wanted us to take off our clothes and underwear. When we wouldn't, he pulled his own down. In fear, I urinated on myself and the bed as my little brother cried, clutching me; trying to hide him behind my four-year-old body, from this dark and confusing moment, this man, now furious, rushed for a bathroom towel, yelling at me, screaming, *"Now look what you've done... You've made a big mess."* Cleaning me up, he fondled me, as my little brother cried and looked on. How I longed for that whistle to blow, and my grandma to come home. I was four years old; my brother was three.

Weekends, my grandmother invited her drinking friend over, Mrs. Meineke. They gathered together regularly, and on one of those nights my brother and I were sent to bed early, as usual. From where I lay I could see straight down the hall to the bathroom, and my grandmother, facing her friend, laughing and drinking. This particular night they were all drunk, and I saw my step-grandfather walk toward the bathroom. When he came out, instead of going back to the "party" he came toward our bedroom.

At first, I thought he was checking to see if we were asleep; *so I pretended to be.* I was wrong. As I continued to pretend sleeping, he pulled my little pajama shorts down and my panties off. From a peek through my eyes I could see that my grandmother was looking off in the other direction. As my step-grandfather would fondle me, I remember thinking, *"Grandma turn around and see."* He placed my tiny feet over his shoulders and proceeded to orally assault me; over and over he would penetrate me in this way; biting me and hurting me. I could feel his face so rough, needing to be shaved; the stubble scraping me raw, would hurt and burn so much. I could, and still can smell the liquor on his breath.

Finally, he returned to the bathroom but, to my surprise, this was not his last visit that night. It turned out to be a very long night for me. I would peek out through my eyes at my grandmother who was carrying on in conversation and drinking. *"Why won't she just turn and see him; why won't she catch him?"* I remember these thoughts rushing through my mind...over and over, so clearly.

> *Jesus loves me, this I know*
> *For the Bible tells me so.*
> *Little ones to Him belong,*
> *They are weak but He is strong.*
> *Yes, Jesus loves me.*
> *Yes, Jesus loves me.*
> *Yes, Jesus loves me.*
> *The Bible tells me so...*

This was to be the only song I would ever remember learning at the Christian daycare where we stayed. As I reflect I see how, *as the seed of the love of Jesus was being planted into my life,* satan the thief came to steal my

6

innocence, my joy and my trust. BUT GOD! His promises remain true and His Word is alive!

And I will also restore for you the years that the locust (destroyer) has eaten . . . JOEL 2:25

Throughout the year, he continued to find ways to get to me. The betrayal I experienced as a four-year-old child was enhanced when I approached my grandmother with the truth, hoping she would help me and the assaults would stop. In the face of my attacker I tall, recalling everything to her. The times we came home late and he carried me to bed from the car sliding his fingers into my panties, fondling me all the way, while my grandmother walked in front of him, to get my bed ready. Countless times I awakened to find him molesting me, penetrating me, kissing my mouth, breathing liquor all over me. The times he would deliberately walk into the bathroom when I was using it. *He had rigged the lock so it would not catch. (I know that now).* How I made myself sick and constipated by not going to use the restroom when my body needed to, for fear he would walk in to watch me; *as a four year old little girl.*

All he could say as I reported all this to my grandmother, as best as a four-year old could, *was that I was lying.* He stood staring me straight in the face and said he had never done it, and she believed him. For whatever reason, she chose to believe him. I was punished and severely disciplined for what they called a lie. He stood, watching as she continued repeatedly, screaming and hitting me. Throwing me into the corner of the room, and threatening to discipline me more if I ever spoke of it to anyone again; ***I was silenced.*** I was told no one would believe a liar; *and the molestations continued.*

My mother eventually came for us. One day, she arrived and running into her arms, I can recall wanting, *almost immediately remembering,* to tell her everything. Too quickly I reminded myself of my grandmother's words and warning: *"no one would ever believe a little liar like you."* This form of abuse did not end with my step-grandfather.

The curse of destruction that had entered through the attacks of incest followed me throughout my life. As if something had attached itself to me. At the age of six, cousins and our babysitter's brother sexually molested me, exposing me to various forms of cruel molestations. At the age of twelve the brother of my stepmother also molested me, in his own home. Another of her brothers, cornered me in my own father's house, and yet a third brother of hers would later stalk me, and come to my job, for five years. My early years were very unstable.

By the time I reached the 10ᵗʰ grade, I had been in eight schools. My mother had remarried, started a family with her new husband in San Antonio, Texas, while my daddy had done the same with his new wife in Houston. I felt out of place with my mother, as many young mother/daughter relationships can be. I moved between these two families for several years, never really establishing any roots, until I finally ended up with my dad, in Houston.

This arrangement did not suit my new stepmother who was very bitter toward me for different reasons. She and my mother had known each other as children. They, and my dad and stepdad had all grown up together and gone to the same schools in Hondo. Whenever she looked at me, she saw my mother, whom I resemble very strongly. It was during these years that I was molested by her brother at the age of twelve. Fearing a reaction similar to what was experienced only eight years earlier, I failed to say anything. Her attitude toward me further fueled my silence, keeping everything to myself.

Even the day my half-sister and I skipped our summer job, to go hang out at a *new friend's* house; after getting into the liquor cabinet, we decided to walk to the store several blocks away.   At fourteen, I found myself alone with this new friend, and suddenly walking through the middle of a baseball field; *the middle of my storm.* I remember it was a hot humid Houston day, and we were walking through this overgrown field, with the grass up to my shoulders. Turning to ask him where we were going, this boy 16 years of age who I believed to be *no-threat,* kept silent and kept walking. I didn't feel threatened, and just figured he hadn't heard me; he was a "good" friend of mine, but I didn't know he had drugged my beverage. Suddenly as we were walking, I recall being grabbed by him from behind, very forcefully.   He threw me on the ground and pounced on me, before I knew what was happening, and began taking my pants off.   I remember struggling with him and telling him to stop. Fighting him as hard as I could, my arms felt weighted and my world was spinning. Fire ants began to cover me, running all over my arms, neck and face, crawling up my shirt all over me, biting me; I remember way off in the distance a small plane flying over us as he raped me. I kept everything to myself. *No one would believe me anyway.*

During the three years of living in my dad's home, there was constant turmoil with my stepmother, who continued to see to it that there was a continual divider at home between myself and my dad, or her daughter from a previous marriage.   I began to stay away from home as much as possible, attempting to stay out of her way. The last thing I wanted was to have my dad in the middle of constant turmoil. My father still had the effects of the shrapnel/bullet fragments embedded in his head! To this day, he suffers from the trauma of Viet-Nam.

Feeling rejected and cast out, I went seeking affection from boys my age. As before, there was no one to guide me. It was not that my parents or other family members failed to tell me they loved me, it was that I never *felt the love they professed to have for me.* Arguments at home intensified and I rebelled.

Many years of tormenting self-blame, and inferiority followed. With a great sense of unworthiness and ugliness, I blamed myself for failed relationships. The rejection I learned to receive as a child, followed me now into every adult relationship. I wanted so very much to be loved, to know **how to love** and *how to allow myself to be loved.* Reaching out for love only brought on spurning rejection in the end. Then there were the times where I set myself up for rejection, by my own fears; ruled by a *fear of rejection.*

My entire life was one of defeat...*until the day,* several years later, when I fell into the arms of the only One who could free me; Jesus Christ. There was no one I believed I could trust, male or female for fear of being betrayed. I had absolutely no confidence in people, fearing they all would turn against me...and in truth, they did in many ways. Jesus healed that area of my life as well, when I gave Him all that pain and insecurity.

I was hungry for acceptance, thirsty for love in a place where none could truly be expressed. With only bits of dry, *brittle confidence* I learned to quickly push away, remove myself or just shut-down. No matter where I turned, I found only bitter resentment from others who claimed affection. Those who were able to give this love I sought after were too busy with their lives, to help me.

I am the Bread of Life.
He who comes to Me will never be hungry,
and he who believes in Me and trusts in Me
will never thirst anymore (at any time).

JOHN 6:35

CHAPTER TWO

HUSBANDS,
LOVE YOUR WIVES

YEAR 1980

𝒪ut of rebellion, I ran away from home at the age of 16, only to learn I was now four months pregnant. I believed this boy when he said he loved me. Maybe it was out of a desperate need to be loved. I did not want to marry him, though, but wanted to finish school and work part-time to provide for my child; *but no one would tell me I could.*

By my seventh month, I was married in absolute anger, humility and shame to a "man" who had already started showing signs of abuse. Two weeks before we married, he kicked me in the lower part of my back with steel-toe boots, bruising me around my kidneys. Giving in to insecurity and fear of rejection I convinced myself that he would change once we married. I had hopes and dreams for my soon-to-be husband and baby.

Within days of marrying, his temper would flare at the slightest impulse. I made excuses for him, thinking he was under so much strain and tried harder each day to please him. He screamed in hatred to me, every day, but I would tell myself he would fall in love with me soon...convince myself and would believe his heart would change toward me, this time thinking our baby would bring him all the happiness I could not give him.

During my eighth month of pregnancy, he held a five-inch switchblade to my belly, and alternated blows to my face and head with the butt of the blade and his fist, as he tried to run over three other people. Escaping while the car was pausing at a stop sign, I ran for my life and that of my unborn baby, jumping ditches and running through neighborhoods at the wee-hours of the morning; it was 2.m., and he didn't want to go home from the party. When our daughter, Anissa was newly born and only days old, he lifted me off the floor by my hair and threw me to the ground. Repeatedly kicking me, he ruptured my birth stitches.

When she was three months old he chased me with a gun. Running from him with my crying daughter clutched in my arms, I hid in the very back of a garage behind a load of boxes and under a pile of old clothes, sweaty, scared and confused...crying because I could not even figure out what I had done to make him so mad at me, *this time.* As I hid, in such fear for my baby, I could hear him yelling just outside the garage that if he "found me, he would kill me." Cursing me with every known defaming profanity he could think of, and some he made up, he swore death over me. When I heard the police, I cried as they arrested him, because I saw more and more clearly, how my dreams were fading away. I could not stand the reality of this toxic, dysfunctional marriage and continued making excuses for him...*but he only grew worse.*

Many times, throughout our nine months of living together in absolute hell, I had knots all over my head, busted mouth and bruises covering my face, arms and legs. He hit me so hard, knocking my jawbone so sharply that the pain would last for weeks. I would beg him not to hit me, and he would

13

just tell me to shut up, that I was stupid and ugly; that no one ever would ever love me; *and I believed him.*

After my eighteenth birthday, in the middle of the street late at night, he beat me because he was out of drugs. My daughter was five months old, in my arms, and screaming in hysterical fear; *I was also three months pregnant with my second child.* As I clutched my baby close to me, he held my head in place with his hand clutching my hair. I held my baby with both arms and hands covering her little head... while his grip was so great, my scalp popped at the skull each time he punched me full force, square in the face. As if that were not enough, he used a board, a cut 2x4, and rammed it at the gap between my nose and left eye, causing it to shut instantly, for three weeks. He beat me until I was nearly unconscious; I was then dragged by my hair, over broken glass that was scattered on the driveway, still holding my screaming baby with both hands over her head. I was completely in the power of his grip. Defenseless.

For the Lord, God of Israel, says, I hate
divorce and marital separation <u>and him</u>
<u>who covers his wife with violence.</u> MALACHI 2:16

He delivers me from my enemies. Yes, you lift me up
above those that rise up against me: you have delivered
(freed) me from the violent man. PSALM 18:48

I know what it is to be stripped of your innocence and confidence by someone you love, or want to love, very much; to have every hope shattered, and every prayer spit on. What it ***is to be*** torn and disowned, I know very well. For more than any of that I know what it is to be utterly restored not only from a traumatic childhood, *but also from the violent man.* Jesus has restored my very soul (Psalm 23:3). He is the only One Who knows what you have gone through, the depth of that place. God did not do it, nor did He allow it. The one who comes to steal, to kill and destroy, is satan.

> *The thief comes only to steal, kill and destroy. I, [Jesus] came that you may have and enjoy life, and have it in abundance (full till it overflows).* JOHN 10:10

So much of what happened was due to poor judgment. Trusting people who we do not always know cannot be trusted can sometimes prove to be very harmful. This is what happened when my mother chose to live life in the fast lane, giving satan every opportunity to come against us. She saw no reason why she *could not* trust leaving us to the care of her mother and step-father, **but this is what opened the door to a curse over us...***the curse of destruction.*

If she had known, of course I know her decision would have been completely different. God has warned us in His Word that by *not knowing* His will for us, and the promises and guiding wisdom provided for us in His Word, we will certainly perish.

> *My people are destroyed for lack of knowledge; seeing you have rejected knowledge, I will also reject you, that you shall be no priest to me; seeing you have forgotten the law of your God, I will also forget your children.* HOSEA 4:6

This declares we are destroyed for a lack of knowledge. By not knowing God's will, and His Word, we open ourselves up to destructive circumstances and situations. We inherit the curses that are passed to us through our parents' and grand-parents' sins. Sins committed by them in their lack of knowing God's Word. Curses that will only be broken from our lives when we take a step **forward** in life and **choose** to live God's **way.**

Satan is the one who told you *God is the One to blame for all the pain and the heartache you have suffered.* He attacks everyone that is precious to God. Satan is a liar and the father of all lies; for it is written to those who oppose God...

> *You are of your father, the devil, and it is your will to practice the lust and gratify the desires (which are known to be) of your father. He was a murderer from the start, and does not stand in the truth for there is no truth in him. When he speaks a lie, he speaks what is natural to him, for he is a liar (himself) and the father of lies and of all that is false.* JOHN 8:44

Many months I blamed God. The only argument I had was, "Well, God, if you're so good and you love me so much, *why did you let this happen to me?*" Now I know the truth of who was the cause of all the grief in my life...**this truth has made me free.**

> *And you will know the truth, and the Truth shall make you free.*
> JOHN 8:32

The spirit of destruction was upon my home and upon my life. Thank God for Jesus...through Him, and Him only is the curse reversed! He purchased our total, complete freedom from the curse of the Law and its condemnation, as He Himself became a curse for us, hanging at Calvary on the cross in our place; He took pain, betrayal, grief, sorrow, rejection, and so much more.

*Christ purchased our freedom (by redeeming us) from
the curse of the Law (in its condemnation) by Himself
becoming a curse for us, for it is written, cursed is
everyone who hangs on a tree (is crucified).*
GALATIANS 3:13

What is this Law? God's Law states that the penalty for sin is
death.

*For the law of the Spirit of life, in Christ Jesus,
(the law of our new being) has freed me from the
law of sin and of death.* ROMANS 8:2

Jesus became our sin as he took upon Himself all curses,
and dying in our place, reconciled us to God. In becoming
the final sacrifice for all sin, He saved us from the wrath of
God, bringing us to right standing with the Father; He raised
us to a position of power, authority, and righteousness in
Himself, before God. **Now because of the Blood** He shed
and through prayer, we can come into the presence of God.
God will never send us to hell; *we send ourselves by denying
Jesus the only opportunity to transform our lives.*

*God did not send the Son into the world to
judge the world but so the world might find salvation and
be made safe and sound through Him. Whoever will
believe in Him, (trust and rely on Him) is not judged
(condemned, rejected, not damned).* **But he who does
not believe in Him is judged already for he has not
believed in the Name of the only begotten Son of
God. (He is damned for refusing to trust in the
name of Christ).** JOHN 3:17,18

How often we mistakenly imagine that we can one day stand

17

before God and *talk our way out of hell.* Our thoughts, and actions, purposes and intentions will all come before us as we stand before the God of all Creation. The only thing He will be looking for is the shed Blood of Jesus Christ that washes away all our sins, when we ask Him to be our Lord. Nothing will be hidden from Him on that day. Believing in Him while there is still time is what will make all the difference in whether we make it into heaven, or send ourselves to hell.

The truth is that God did love me so much He sent Jesus Christ, His only Son, to take all my sins away when I accepted His life's sacrifice, so I would not go to hell forever separated from God. **The very One Who did this for me, also did it for the man who so bitterly betrayed me. God has no favorites.** He loves us all, but it is the sins we commit that keep us separate from Him. **He loves us, *not our sin.*** His love covers all sin without a trace left; He promises never again to bring it up once it has been forgiven. We are not strong enough to carry the burden of sin anyway, but He is. How wonderful to know that God has provided the One True Way to inner peace. *How sad, that too many still don't find it...*

I not only needed to be freed from the sins I had committed myself but also from the sins others had committed ***against me.*** **These were sins against my soul.** Sins that went deeper than those I had committed against myself.

Nothing is too hard for God!

CHAPTER THREE

LIVING IN THE FLESH

YEAR 1984

$\mathcal{A}$t the end of my first marriage, I turned to world of nightclubs and the fast lane. I had divorced my first husband, married a man in San Antonio was expecting the birth of our child (my third), when he had an affair. Aside from the shock and pain, and everything that goes along with rejection, I knew the marriage was over and left with my babies.

Alone to raise three children, ages five months, one year and a two-year-old, I returned to Houston with a limited education and no job training....I was *a 10th grade drop-out with a GED after my first husband refused to allow me to go back to school.* All I could do was answer phones and type about 25 words per minute. My work experience was zero; I received no child support, *and had no direction.* Alone with three babies, I quickly learned how to make fast money as a dancer. *This was one of satan's traps.* Every six to eight months, I was able to find a clerical job paying no more than five dollars an hour. This didn't last very long, being a *single parent with two in diapers.*

I was enslaved to this kind of humiliating self-abuse and entrapment for four years. I had come to trust men *less and* *less, and liked them **even less.*** Surrounded by men gazing or lusting, smirking and some ignoring me...I tried to make a living, and I tried to survive. My self-image was very poor, but each time I took the stage, I couldn't allow others to see what I really thought of myself. I'll never know how many faces I looked into **daily,** often wondering if the man of my dreams had *finally come* to rescue me from this misery.

Coming face to face with what I had become was too much for me to handle on my own. This is when I learned other loved ones were now being sexually molested by a family member.

I began to drink extensively, daily, and began to experiment with cocaine. I saw myself as never having a decent, well-paying job. I saw how impossible it was for me to ever have a man love me in all purity, or even allow myself to be loved. I became untouchable, avoiding more pain. A wall of defense surrounded me, and no one was allowed in. I played the part of a self-fulfilled single woman, putting on an act, pushing myself to fit in. The drugs and alcohol helped me play the part better, but inside I was literally torn, and devastated. ***On the outside I was the life of the party; but on the inside, I was dying.***

Many nights I left with other men in total ignorance. It was a miracle that I was never harmed. There were many times I was chased on the freeway, shot at by jealous men; other times I would get home at 3:00 a.m. to find someone was lurking in my back yard. When I lived in an upstairs apartment, thinking it to be safer, I learned one man was climbing the back part of the building trying to enter my back window. This same man prowled on the roof watching me as I came and went, making several attempts to enter my home, for months.

Now I was being stalked.

Countless times I slept at the foot of the front door to my apartment, after having the locks rigged by this stalker; several times during the night, he tried to open the door only to find I was blocking it with my body while my babies slept in their room. I had no phone. I soon learned this stalker was the same man who had held me at knifepoint (butcher knife) overnight; a man from my past. A man who I had escaped from, *once before.*

For three weeks, I lived in my car with all three children, after this stalker forced me out of my home; he attacked me inside a convenience store, ripping my keys from my hands... the police knew my lifestyle, so with smirks and sarcasm they took my report and sent us on our way. *There was no help for someone like me.*

So many times, I attempted to leave this life of corruption, lies and emptiness but no one would point the way of help to me. My daddy condemned, and cursed me saying I was not his daughter. For over two years he refused to speak to me at all. My mother also refused many times to help me with even one child. I wanted to go to school, and get an education...be someone for my kids; but no one would help me. My college was secured! I was headed to West Point Academy... *what happened?*

No one came around and said "Hey, I care...let me help you; let me point the way". What I did receive were insults aimed at my children! *How I yearned to be free...*

Hear my cry, O God; listen to my prayer. From the end of the earth I cry out to You. When my heart is over-whelmed, and fainting lead me to the rock that is so much

higher than I, yes, to a rock that is too high for me.
PSALM 61: 1, 2

In 1986, a foreign man came to the club. It was rare for me *not* to leave with a man, since I needed the extra money...but this man tried without any success for months. Not until the night he came offering to support me and my children in every financial area, *on the condition I stop working these clubs.* My income had decreased as a result of the state of depression I was in.

I saw this man as my way out of the nightclubs. Several months passed as he proposed marriage to me, only to learn he was already married with children of his own in his Caribbean country. He was a lead man for drug traffickers, whose main connections ran throughout Mexico, Texas, New York, South America as well as all over the United States.

I soon began my career as a model in commercial print. My experience quickly lead me into the glamorous world of television commercials for make-up, local ads in newspapers for fitness, national swimsuit magazines and winning the title of 1987 Spokes Model in the Texas Star Search Competition. Like many little girls, it had been a dream of mine as a child but without honest, true professionals leading me, it wasn't long before the referrals I received, by a backslid Christian modeling agent, began to go through an individual who was steering me into pornography; *who had an eye for my children.*

Contracts for music videos, commercial print for local gyms and make-up, came quickly but with hidden motives; learning the price that was going to be expected of me, I soon realized the direction I was headed in; *I had just left this scene a year earlier.* My drug addiction increased with the levels of depression, to the point where I no longer had an interest in my work. I dropped out of the 1988 Texas Star Search Competition leading in all categories, a week before the final judging. I was too "wired" on cocaine to care.

At the peak of my addiction, I used no less than $500 a day of pure (stolen) cocaine. In three short years, the relationship ended with that man and my career fizzled. In addition, I had aborted three unplanned, pregnancies.

Abortion is horrible. The taking of human life is beyond a doubt hideous in itself... *but to deliberately stop the heartbeat of an unborn child.* A child, never given the chance to take the first breath of life, can only gasp as life is sucked out and the body broken apart. One cell at a time; one piece at a time.

They *(those who perform these abortions),* don't tell you that. They don't show you the pictures, going in. They don't call it **what it is.** They just take your money, and put you at the back of the line. A long line of women who are all there for the same thing; *no other men around.* Where are the men who helped get these women to this place, *was my question?* Many people argue the unborn baby (fetus) is living; but that does not change the truth...

*My frame was not hidden from You, when I was being formed in secret; Your eyes saw my **unformed substance** and in Your book, all the days of my life were written before ever they took shape, when as yet there was none of them.* PSALM 139: 15, 16

The fear of raising another child on my own overwhelmed me, while my need for love consumed me through **selfishness.** There will be a day in the Kingdom of God that

I will face these babies, and they will look at me with the love of God, pure and true. *With forgiveness.*

My heart looks forward to that day...

Each time I went to an abortion clinic, *another part of me died;* and each time as I lay on the clinical operating table *I cried uncontrollably.* It was never my desire to allow the life of my child to be taken; *but I was afraid and I was alone.* I knew I was wrong in what I was doing, <u>but I had no faith.</u> Nor did I have any knowledge of God. My family and friends failed to support me emotionally, and I made some of the worst decisions of my entire life. BUT GOD IS FAITHFUL TO FORGIVE US WHEN WE ASK.

How desperately important it is to have a knowledge of God, *personally.* Just to know Him more intimately, and knowing His unconditional forgiveness is what makes the difference in our lives. There can be no substitute for His presence, His strength and His forgiveness. Nothing can measure up to the mercy of God. There is nothing this world has to offer that can wash the stain of sin and guilt from our lives. A priceless gift of Blood was given, in the exchange for our freedom. Not just any blood... the Blood of a sinless Man named Jesus Christ was poured out willingly in His love for us. Mine was the sin of a willful, contrary and rebellious spirit. He shed His Blood for me to be forever forgiven, of that!

In addition to cocaine, I was also addicted to marijuana, Darvon, Motrin and Soma along with at least three bottles a week of Maximum Strength Tylenol. In order to come off my *"high"* I would ingest several drugs that would bring me "down", rapidly. I soon experienced two near heart attacks before the age of twenty-four. I was hitting on cocaine every five minutes or less *in the absolute loss of hope.*

Many times, I could hear voices. Countless times I would be on the bathroom floor pulling on my own hair in sheer madness. I can't remember how many times I wanted to end my own life. In my own eyes, I could not see an end to my pain. It was a pain that no pill, no drug, no doctor could relieve. *It was the pain of a broken heart. The pain of a shattered soul.*

Throughout this period of grief and total loss of identity, my mind played back the painful memories of assault as a child. Each time. Every detail. Without warning, and uninvited the memories would invade whatever it was I was doing...

It was November 1987, and suicide became a *very familiar* thought that *I entertained.* I had not realized how often my thoughts played with those thoughts or *considered how life for my loved ones would be without me.* I never considered the devil wanted to influence my mind and heart. That it was evil behind the racing thoughts I had no control over; and how my emotions were going unchecked. I had spiraled. I had closed myself in. I was dying, very slowly, again.

The following entry is taken from my personal journal during a period of sheer darkness, just one month prior to the first suicide attempt. *Christmas was coming...*

PRINCESS

I cried for mama late at night when no one was around.
Think of the emptiness I felt, when she could not be found.

The princess is alone again, except for baby brother.
Grandma's drinking with her friend,
and here comes her grandfather.

He's not her real grandpa, see,
so maybe that is why...
he sneaks into her room at night
and makes the princess cry.

I can remember late at night,
you did the things I knew weren't right.

"Pretend to be asleep", I'd tell myself,
"He'll go away."
He'd think no one was watching,
so longer, he would stay.

When morning came, T'was like a dream,
all that happened didn't seem
so real anymore,
except my panties on the floor.

The years have come and gone its true,
50 years in all.
The hurt inside my soul is deeper
than when I was small.
For now I understand what happened
to a child of four,
whose innocence was stolen
by a heartless man who swore,
"That children lie most everyday"
as grandma turned and walked away.

She chose to love a man who lied,
and to her grandchild, love denied.
A child who spoke of what she'd learned,
taught by a lonely man who yearned.

So now you know that I recall
the choice you made when I was small,

> *to overlook my trust in you*
> *as you did things you longed to do.*
>
> *I can remember late at night,*
> *you did the things I knew weren't right.*

I was now *so utterly grief stricken; thoughts of death filled my mind.* Before long I had developed an interest in white magic, foolishly thinking there was a difference between white and black magic. By reading books on white magic alone, I opened the door to witchcraft and the occult **on myself.** The following is taken from my personal journal, less than a week prior to a second suicide attempt. I had been awake three days and nights on cocaine and gallons of hard liquor. Early, on entering the fourth morning with no food or water, only the drugs and alcohol, I sat on the floor of my bathroom with a tray of cocaine on the toilet lid, ready.

This entry was made December 5, 1987:

*I can remember all of it. My eyes hurt. Christmas is here; that's when it all began. My eyes hurt. I just want to sleep. But I can remember everyone... Everyone. **Everything.** Now I lay me down to sleep. I pray the Lord my soul to keep. If I should die before I wake...**or is it wake before I die?** Before I die; maybe I'll reach it. It's too much. There's too much. I can't anymore. What happens when your heart breaks? Does it stop? Is that the only way? I have to stop... Stop... Just stop. Remember what you used to do to me? Remember? Remember? Remember, Remember...!*

I REMEMBER!!!

I hate.　　　　　　　There's no more time.
I hope.　　　　　　　　I want to go away.
I cry.　　　　　　　No one has to know.
I hope...　　　　　　everything will change.
I listen.　　　　　　Everyone will cry...
I write.　　　　　　　　　　　　Cry
　I write.　　　　　　　　　　Cry
　　and write some more.　　　Cry
　　No one will listen.　　　Cry
　　　No one else understands.　Cry

WANT: PEACE OF MIND

There's no balance. I'm lost.
I'm in my own little corner.
You can't cross this line.
The walls are too high now.
I can't handle much anymore.
I'm lost.

Yes, I'm lost...

Come to Me, all you who labor...
and are heavy-laden...and overburdened,
and I will cause you to rest.
(I will ease, relieve and refresh your souls).
MATTHEW 11:28

CHAPTER FOUR

THE DEAD SHALL HEAR HIS VOICE

YEAR 1987

In my darkest, hour, when it appeared nothing could happen to worsen my mental condition, I discovered I was again going to have a baby. I had been living with a man and we were both alcoholics and drug addicts. We did not want another child nor did we want to get married. He also had three children from his first failed marriage, *as I did.*

I was desperate **not to have** a child or **go through another** clinical abortion, and in the state of mind I was in I chose to take an overdose of drugs; thinking it would flush my baby out of my body. Only six weeks into my pregnancy, I sought the only way out I knew.

I had been awake for over three days again, with no type of food at all; cocaine had become my food and I consumed this along with other drugs, in larger quantities. In an effort to induce my own miscarriage, a "drug buddy" came to me with a home remedy that insured a miscarriage; she was a registered nurse, and cocaine addict.

I went into my bathroom, proceeding to drink this mixture, and immediately my blood pressure dropped drastically, and my entire body began convulsing. I could feel myself jerking on the floor; I could see the very bottom of the sink vanity, and where I had not swept... but I could not stop or get up. As quickly as it started, it stopped and after a short period of time, I picked myself up off the floor, glancing toward the mirror, only to see the ugliest pale gray reflection of death glaring back... *but God called out to me!*

In His mercy, and in His sheer love and compassion, *He called out to me! Me,* the drug addict who had committed the very act of abortion not once, but many times; *Me...* the one who had prostituted herself for money and drugs. *He called out to me!* and said, "SANDRA, YOU WILL HAVE THIS CHILD". Don't ask me how I know it was God; all I can say is <u>I know, that I know, that I know</u> *it was God. A voice so firm, yet gentle... a voice of pure pulsating love; of peace, and calm in the middle of my storm. I was far from God. I didn't even believe in God!!!*

*Believe Me when I assure you, most solemnly I tell you, the time is coming and is here now <u>when the dead shall hear the voice of the Son of God,</u> **and those who hear it** shall live.*
JOHN 5:25

As quickly as I could get myself to the front room I told my boyfriend, who agreed with me, and we flushed all remaining $5,000-$6,000 worth of cocaine down the toilet. I dreaded the thought of withdrawal because I had experienced it before many times, but God... in His mercy and sheer compassion removed every trace of drugs from my system and I didn't go through any form of withdrawal at all. I don't recall the pain of it, this time.

I had never known God. I made a few attempts at returning to different churches, but that didn't last. *I was searching.* Within months, though, I experienced changes in my

31

appearance. My hair began to fall out very easily; my skin was also turning color. I knew something was very wrong; my body, my skin was infected, purple, blotched and bleeding.

As a model, I daily visited tanning salons or was out at the beach or pool, sunbathing. Daily for hours, *taking no precautions,* I soon overexposed myself to the sun and salons. I went to many doctors, who knew nothing of my addiction to drugs, and underwent several tests including for the HIV virus. My skin condition worsened with no explanation, at first.

Huge welted spots appeared over the back of my body the size of a tennis shoe and covered my arms, legs, stomach, face, neck, everywhere. My hair began to fall out in large quantities and it was impossible for me to shower, or even sponge bathe, for such excruciating pain. The drugs caused a major imbalance internally, due to the chemical poisoning I had exposed myself to. It was as if I were burned on the outside *and on the inside* of my body.

My body was *wracked with pain.* For someone to touch me, even gently, was unbearable. I was on the verge of a nervous breakdown. Trapped, *encased in a shell of burning pain.* Intense, non-stop itching covered my body. This itching was beneath my skin, and I tried to find relief scraping myself so raw, until I no longer had fingernails. Other times I would use a coarse brush, a loofa sponge, or knife tip, in a mad attempt to gain relief from this severely tormenting burning-itch. My skin bled, was completely sore and raw from repeated scraping and clawing off the layers of my flesh. *I still have the scars. Battle scars!*
I developed sores at the base of my neck, elbows and behind my knees. I was literally purple with soreness from the constant scraping, and my flesh began to smell like rotted

meat. In bed, my skin would stick to the sheets, pillow cases, and clothing. My skin cells, reproducing the way a scraped knee would, only all at once, left a sticky-gooey substance all over my body. Each time I rolled in bed, or got up, I would have to peel off the sheets or pillowcases from my body and face, as the new skin would dry onto the fabric, when I'd fall asleep.

In June of 1988 at 6 months of pregnancy, my doctor removed me from all medication seeing no progress in my condition. Referred to the University of Texas Health Science Center for testing and research, his only remark to me was that I had a form of cancer... I had already gone through over 10 doctors at the Diagnostic Clinic in Houston's Medical Center; Hematologists, Dermatologists and other specialists in nervous disorders.

My obstetrician was very concerned for my unborn child. He constantly spoke of his fear for the development of my baby, but I refused to believe in my heart anything negative spoken. I would only speak what I wanted to see for my child. Everything my body had been through, the drugs, abortions and this spreading evil over my entire body, caused him to believe I would lose my baby before full term or my child would be born severely malformed or brain damaged.

But the Lord, in His absolute mercy and sheer compassion had other plans... and I have come to learn that God's plans are the ones that prevail!

> *Many plans are in a man's mind, but it is the Lord's purpose for him, that will stand.* PROVERBS 19:21

I knew I had heard from God before, but *I wanted something I could see, and something I could feel.* God's

Word says that without faith you cannot please God in any way. Faith is not something you see, faith is what you believe and hope for, knowing you receive it... *and without a doubt.* Faith steadfastly holds on to the end without wavering. I knew nothing about *"walking by faith and not by sight"*. I had to **unlearn the bad habit** of *"seeing is believing"*. **I had to unlearn that lie,** and instead learn sight through the *eyes of faith.* Seeing what I hoped for, and believing I already had it, until I held or physically received it, *without doubt and without being double minded.*

The trap of needing something to see or touch, in order to believe, is how the witchcraft snared me. In my lack of knowledge of God's will for my life I sought the dark side of the supernatural.

During my pregnancy and the sickness that covered me I was simultaneously involved in the occult practices of witchcraft and demonology. *I was lured to believe the lie that there was a difference between white and black magic.* It was not long before white magic was not enough and I entered the darker world of voodoo, the study of demons, channeling, crystals, tarot cards and biorhythm, astrology, use of charms, transcendental meditation, self-hypnosis. I could audibly hear voices that no one else could hear. Voices not only of anger but vengeance, and sometimes those of grief, or jealousy. Many times, I was carrying on a conversation with voices that, at first, I brushed off as *"talking to myself",* when I was really conversing with demons... familiar spirits that were known to attend a witch; the same demons I had invited into my life *unaware* when chanting spells of witchcraft.

I often visited the homes of witches and psychics, believing they could direct me and guide me. *Psychics are nothing more than witches.* They choose to call themselves psychics because most of society shuns the word *"witch"* but will accept the word "psychic". Psychics operate with familiar spirits (demons). That is where they get their "knowledge". They'll tell you just enough to snare you; I know because I practiced occultism diligently and snared many people. I was so deceived. For months, I became more entangled in a web of darkness.

> *My people are destroyed for lack of knowledge...*
> *HOSEA 4:6*

Through ignorance and lack of true knowledge, I practiced witchcraft. One reason was for prosperity, when actually I *was losing all I had;* selling, and pawning everything I owned *until I had nothing left. Now my health was deteriorating.*

It was my mother who began to pray, after first warning me of *going off the deep end* when she learned I was using crystals and channeling. Another family member, a (Holy) Spirit filled Christian, knew of the witchcraft I was practicing.

She would encourage me to stop *living in a sinful life of adultery. In the eyes of God, "I was unclean and His Holy anger was upon me"* she said, and she was right!

> *So, kill evil desires lurking in your members (within you):*
> *sexual vice, impurity, sensual appetites, and unholy desires,*
> *all greed, covetousness that is idolatry. It is on account of*
> *these sins that the holy anger of God is upon the sons of*
> *disobedience. COLOSSIANS 3:5, 6*

> *For from within, out of the heart, come base and wicked*
> *thoughts, sexual immorality, stealing, murder, adultery,*
> *coveting (that is a greedy desire for wealth), deceit,*
> *dangerous, and destructive wickedness, unrestrained,*
> *indecent conduct; an evil eye (envy), slander, pride (the sin*

of an uplifted heart against God and man), foolishness (lack of sense, thoughtlessness); all these evils come from within, and they make the man unclean. MARK 7:21-23

Then He said to His disciples, the harvest is indeed plentiful, but the laborers are few. So, pray the Lord of the harvest to **force out and thrust** *laborers into His harvest.*
MATTHEW 9:37, 38

An early September morning, three months after being released from my primary physician, I went into labor, continuing to suffer the pain of the disease. I had carried my child full term, which was half the battle, but complications rose up against us, with the threat of emergency surgery. I had never really learned how to pray, but I prayed the only way I knew how. I said *"Jesus, save my baby; let him be normal, and I promise to go to church every week".* This was pretty much all I prayed... *but God...* He knew my heart. Nothing can ever be hidden from Him.

The hearing ear and the seeing eye,
the Lord has made both of them.
PROVERBS 20:12

He sees all, He hears all, and He knows all. Nothing is hidden from Him. He is God!

The doctor ordered my prepping for surgery to be in an hour. I called everyone who I knew who could pray... and in exactly thirty minutes, with half an hour left until my operation, my son was born! The hand of God was on this baby, and after only fifteen hours from the time of his birth we were released to go home!

The Lord *restored laughter* to me through Isaac, *which means laughter...* and this little messenger of God (Gabriel) renewed hope as he entered my life, *healthy!* I witnessed the power of prayer as he was born, and knew there was a God of mercy. I wanted to know God, but didn't know how to find Him. My desire for Him didn't fade, although I gave up easily when I failed to tap into His power. He was not about to lower Himself to my terms. I had to make it right with God. I had to make things right in my life. It was time to make the *wrong thing, right!*

CHAPTER FIVE

DRAWING NEAR
TO GOD

YEAR 1989

𝒯he following six months lingered with little change. Even though we tried to seek the Lord, we did it on our terms, continuing to live together, dabbling in the occult, and playing with the grace of God. My physical condition worsened and again, suicidal thoughts and impressions came to play. I could only think of my children, as they had only me. How would they survive if something so horrible were to happen? Who would care for them? Was there anyone?

My boyfriend was raised in a dysfunctional, violent home. His grandfather was a necromancer, raising him in the demonic world of communicating with the dead and demon spirits, allowing himself to be used as a channel.

There shall not be found among you anyone who will
make his son, or daughter pass through the fire or who
uses divination, or soothsayer, or an auger, sorcerer,
charmer, medium, wizard or necromancer.
For all these things is an abomination to the Lord.
DEUTERONOMY 18:10-12

Grandparents on both sides of his family were either spiritist-mediums or witches. He would have to make a firm decision to serve the Lord, in order to break the curse, *the cycle of sin and death,* that was on his family's lineage. All he knew was rejection, violence, and neglect. He did not know love. He doesn't remember ever being told he was loved. *He had never known love.* But the plans of the Lord prevail!

> *For I know the thoughts and plans that I have for you,*
> *says the Lord, thoughts and plans for goodness*
> *and peace and not for evil, to give you hope in your*
> *final outcome (future).* JEREMIAH 29:11

One afternoon, we fought terribly. Tormented voices raced through my mind continually. I was in the bathroom literally losing my mind, with my entire body encased in excruciating pain. Desiring death again over this life of anguish, I clutched, and pulled my hair in torment, crying in agony. I had no medical help whatsoever; no one to call for help.

A still, small voice could faintly be heard... *"You will live,"* is all I was told. **"You Will Live!"** This was not a voice of anger, but of love; not of the turmoil that was *darting* me through voices of hate, but of peace...*and of hope. A silent voice,* if you will. The peaceful voice of God during the turmoil that raged through my mind.

Anger was loosed often in our home, as I gave in to its taunting voice. Storming from one room to another throwing things, bashing holes into walls, or with a broom handle destroy everything in the kitchen, no one knew the root of my anger was *"fear"* of loss.

One argument ended when my boyfriend tried to escape by jumping out the bedroom window, from our second-floor apartment. Pulling him back by his belt strap, he ran through the front door, down the staircase as I threw a bar-b-que pit, striking him.

I've been lifted off the floor by my throat, and crushed against the bathroom vanity with a broken tip of a chopstick, threatening to shove up my nose and *"tickle my brain."* The evil of anger will try everything to put hate in your heart for others. The devil will always try his best, but his best is never enough, when you are a child of God; *and I was on my way.*

In early 1989, I gave in to an invitation for some serious prayer at the home of a family member. Desperate and so very tired of my condition, I desired to be free. I wanted to be healed; most of all I really wanted to know Who Jesus Christ was. I was out of hope, but about to find out that Jesus Christ was, and is our only Hope.

I, Paul, an apostle of Christ Jesus
by appointment and by command of God our
Savior and **Christ Jesus...our Hope.** *I TIM. 1:1*

After a series of prayers for freedom from demonic and evil influences and control that had a hold on my life, I began to realize how weak I truly was against those things, and how powerful the grip of sin was in my life. The power of God's Word prayed over me, through the authority of a believer, is what **broke the grip of satan from my life;** when I accepted Jesus Christ as Lord asking Him to free me, to forgive me of all my sins. Sins I could not even remember, **I know** were forgiven that very same moment.

Arriving home, I began to do some spiritual housecleaning; removing everything in my home that was related to witchcraft, the occult, Satanism; $1000's worth of this garbage was finally thrown out of my home; all that had to do with the opposite of God was destroyed, broken or torn. CD's, books, statues of fire gods and other items that are worshipped as gods in other countries, *everything;* and for the very first time in a long time, *there was peace.*

The following morning, preparing to attend Lakewood Church in Houston, Texas, pastored by John and Dodie Osteen, I had no physical evidence of a healing; yet no change was visible, and there was much pain. I could wear no makeup; my face was now infected and puffy, swollen and sore. My hair was falling out and I was more than afraid. Somehow, I managed to get into my car, and smoked marijuana all the way to church. Kicking, arguing, screaming and cussing, we were going to church, for the first time together. *We didn't know we were being attacked in the realm of the spirit.* Satan was again up to his tactics, in an effort to cause us such frustration and discouragement so that *we would not go to church at all; so that we would give up! You have to learn to fight through every discouragement that comes your way, in life!*

I continued in rage, screaming that, *"no one in that stupid church was going to want to sit near me. They were all dressed nice and I wasn't ... my hair was falling out and theirs isn't",* and on, and on went my argument, in desperation to *just turn around and not follow through.*

The Presence of God Himself filled the entire place as the door quietly shut behind me, entering the lobby. I became so absolutely awed by what I was experiencing; a pure love, a holiness of perfect love had just absolutely wrapped itself around me as it slapped the marijuana *"high"* right out of me.

No longer dazed state from the drugs, I became distinctly

aware of God's Presence all over me, loving me, knowing me, caressing me. I know now it was the Holy Spirit Himself welcoming me home, as a prodigal child returning for the first time.

The Presence of the Holy Spirit was not only all over, all around me, *but was moving right through me.* I was physically aware of this. I could actually feel the Presence of Someone all over me; I just could not see Him with my natural eyes. As if a cleansing had just begun, He went right through me over and over. I was no longer aware of the strife, only that God was near. I was being transformed inwardly, as the Lord ushered me forward. *I was now on His territory,* in the presence of *His people,* who were all filled with *His Holy Spirit,* and who were all in harmony together to do *His will.* I no longer had thoughts of being out of place...I felt right at home; it was so natural for me to be where I was...in the very Presence of God.

> *Have mercy upon me O God, according to Your*
> *steadfast love; and according to the multitude of Your*
> *tender mercy and loving kindness, blot out my*
> *transgressions. Wash me thoroughly...and repeatedly from*
> *my iniquity and guilt; cleanse me, and make me whole,*
> *purify me from my sin. I am conscious of my sin, it is*
> *forever before me...Purify me and I shall be clean, wash me*
> *and I shall be whiter than snow...Create in me a*
> *clean heart O, God...* PSALM 51: 1–3, 7 and 10

That is exactly what He was doing to me...*washing me, cleansing me, and purifying me.* It felt like being carried on the "wings of the wind", to the main sanctuary of the church. I saw the cameras and flags of the nations and thought it was too commercial; but sat down...as close to the exit as possible, should the need for a quick getaway suddenly arise.

The music started. Such praise and adoration I had never heard before in my life. Hands lifted to the song "Abba, Father", and next I recall a song called, "Something Good is About to Happen", and my hands lifted toward heaven in praise to God, my Father... *I needed a miracle!*

People needing prayer for themselves, others, or sickness, finances, marriage, children; the prayer of agreement, according to the Word of God, *flooded the altar for prayer.*

> *Again, I tell you, if two of you on earth agree,*
> *whatever they ask, it will come to pass and be done*
> *for them by My Father in heaven.*   MATTHEW 18:19

This kind of prayer brings answers *when you mix it with faith;* the childlike faith, of pure and trusting belief, with no doubt whatsoever.

> *And Jesus said...why, all things can be and are*
> *possible to him who believes.*   MARK 9:23

I went for prayer and returned to my seat... *no change.* A woman behind me was led by the Holy Spirit, to share healing scriptures with me...

> *He personally bore our sins in His body on the tree*
> *(cross) that we might die to sin and live righteously.*
> *BY HIS WOUNDS YOU HAVE BEEN HEALED.*
> I PETER 2:24

> *He was wounded for our transgressions, He was*
> *bruised for our guilt and iniquities; the chastisement*
> *(needful to obtain) our peace and well-being was upon Him,*
> *and with the stripes (that wounded) Him we are*
> *healed and made whole.*   ISAIAH 53:5

By the stripes that marked His back, as He was violently whipped so long ago, I can live in divine health today, because Jesus Christ is the same today as He was when He physically walked the earth; He does not change. *Jesus Christ is always the same, yesterday, today and forever.*
HEBREWS 13:8

> *For I am the Lord, I do not change; that is why you... are not consumed.* MALACHI 3:6

The message Pastor Osteen delivered on the morning of March 19ᵗʰ, 1989, as I sat among the congregation, *transformed and sparked hope in me!* The anointing of the Holy Spirit was on his message entitled, *" Turning Tragedy to Triumph". The Spirit of God reached right to the place we were sitting and spoke life to me. Every word of that message was meant for me, *and I welcomed it without delay. I absorbed every word!* Pastor preached that God can bring triumph out of tragedy, but you must be facing a tragedy, before you can get the triumph; *I was.*

He said, "When you're at the end of your rope, jump on over to God's rope". *I was and I did.* He also went on to say, *"Are you saying that all hope is gone? Are you saying I've gone too far"?* Everything that came out of the man of God's mouth pierced my heart. I knew without God, I was doomed. And because of the life that poured through his lips, I now knew I had hope!

> *For the Word that God speaks is alive and full of power; it is sharper than any two-edged sword penetrating to the dividing line of the soul and spirit... exposing and sifting, analyzing and judging the very thoughts and purposes of the heart.* HEBREWS 4:12

The following three weeks were for the trying of my faith. It was not God trying me, He already knew the outcome. Satan was trying to shake my confidence, trying to steal the new Hope I had found, and received in Christ. All I had now was God's Word; I had nothing else in the world to help or strengthen me, *nor did I need anything else. I had LOVE!*

No one could help me; nothing anyone did could help to relieve the searing and agonizing pain that blazed through my body with no end. The closest one to me was my boyfriend, and all he could do for me was pray; *more than doctors had been able to do.* I sat crouched with my arms wrapped around my legs, crying so hard from excruciating pain of the burns on my body. *It felt as if someone had taken sandpaper and had scraped off all my skin.* The pain was unbearable, but with tears, asked the Lord to bring forth quickly, *a miracle of healing into my life. We prayed the Word of God.*

But something was hindering our prayer. It was as if my healing wanted to come... I could see the change wanting to happen, but then a relapse. Even though we were praying God's Word, something was stopping the full effect from coming; hindering the answer from coming!

The mistake I made now was the same as before, *only worse!* I invited Jesus to be the Lord of my life; I had asked for forgiveness and received it instantly but His Word says when He forgives us, **we are to stop sinning or something worse could happen to us.**

Afterward, when Jesus found him in the temple, He said to him, See you are well! Stop sinning or something worse may happen to you. JOHN 5:14

I continued to live together with a man I was not married to, **now** knowing because of the Holy Spirit, that it was wrong. I couldn't continue living this way, with one foot planted in the things of God and one foot in the way of the world. We were not married to each other! To be considered in right-standing with the Lord, we would have to change a lot. God wants what is best for each person, individually. My way of living was only inviting trouble, and hindering my walk with the Lord. The full blessing of the Lord could not be on me for that one detail. I had to choose.

Every valley shall be lifted and filled up, every mountain, and hill shall be made low; and the crooked and uneven shall be made straight and level, the rough places a plain.
ISAIAH 40:4

The valleys (depressed, oppressed people), He shall raise up and fill with His joy. Mountains and hills (proud and arrogant people), He shall bring low and humble. Those who compromise their right standing with God (crooked, uneven), who allow the perverse lifestyle of this evil world to creep into their own lives, God shall make straight and level, the rough places of our spiritual walk will be made plain, as He teaches us to obey the voice of His Spirit, *and not the voice of desire.* Choosing to walk the pathway of a *God-blessed life* can allow no opportunity, or entrance for sin (death), to function, or have place. *The penalty for sin* is death, in the Bible; all that was formerly allowed in our lives *before Christ,* must no longer be allowed to live, to exist within us; God's nature replaces our own. A nature that can only thrive in holy living; righteous living. The righteousness of God, *in Christ Jesus.*

When before, I had found myself in the *pig-pen* of life, I had now made a quality decision to *change every area* of my attitude and my previous way of living and believing!

For so many years, I had lived as a victim of what had happened to me as a child. I could no longer allow the destruction of my past to devastate and destroy my future. Sexual abuse, sexual assault, namely *Incest and rape for me* had literally bred destruction in every event of my life. But now, the tide of the battle was turning. **God was invading my storm, and bringing me through the lost centeredness of it all.** The life-changing, quality decision to live for the Lord, not only in the presence of others, but behind closed doors, was the turning point!

> *Therefore, if any person is in Christ he is a new Creation; the old, (previous moral and spiritual condition) has passed away. Behold the fresh and new has come.* II CORINTHIANS 5:17

He teaches us to obey the
voice of His Spirit,
over the voice of desire.

CHAPTER SIX

THE VIOLENT TAKE
IT BY FORCE

YEAR 1989

A few weeks passed as I hung on to all His promises, diligently searching for more. The pain never lessened, but only intensified; *the difference now was that I stopped saying with my mouth how much it hurt.* I would only thank Him for healing me because His Word declared I was healed, by His sacrifice on the cross. I was learning to agree with God, despite my current condition.

As I thanked Him for my healing in advance of any change, adversity in turn would increase, and the heat of my pain would convince me I was getting worse, I was dying... *God had lied*; but I would refuse to believe those lies. *God was all I had. He was all the Hope I had.* Throughout the searching of His Word I found yet another promise, and applied it to my life...

> *...then the man's flesh shall be restored; it becomes*
> *fresher and more tender than a child's;*
> *he returns to the days of his youth.* JOB 33:25

This promise I combined with others, like the one you will find in the Gospel of Matthew:

*For truly I say to you if you have faith like a grain of
mustard seed you can say to this mountain, move from
here to yonder place, and it will move; and
nothing will be impossible to you.   MATTHEW 17:20*

The Life of God's Word blossomed throughout my very
being. I saw myself through the eyes of the Lord for the first
time in my life. Doing only what was instructed in the Bible,
without any doubt at all, the Word of God became food to
my spirit, and life to my soul.

*... Whoever says to this mountain, be lifted and
thrown into the sea! And does not doubt at all in his heart
but believes that what he says will take place; it will be
done for him.   MARK 11:23*

By the power of the Holy Spirit God had invested in me
when I invited Jesus into my life, I spoke to the mountain of
pain and disease and commanded it to all leave my life and
loose its' hold on me, in the Name of Jesus Christ.

*And whatever you do, in word or deed, do everything
in the Name of the Lord Jesus Christ...giving praise to
God the Father, through Him.   COLOSSIANS 3:17*

I took the authority He had given me found in Luke's
Gospel...

*Behold! I have given you authority and power to tramp-
le upon serpents and scorpions {demons} and (physical,
mental strength and ability) over all the power of the
enemy; and nothing shall in any way harm you.
LUKE 10:19*

I learned that neither sickness, nor anything demonic, would
leave if asked. I forcefully exerted what given authority I had,

and taking what I knew was legally mine in Christ, brought results. I belonged to the Lord. Healing belonged to me, through my Healer.

...the kingdom of heaven has endured violent assault, and violent men seize it by force...
                                    MATTHEW 11:12

Health is of the kingdom of heaven; liberty is of the kingdom of heaven, as is prosperity and wholeness in every area of life. We do not have to wait until we get to heaven before we can enjoy all of this either... we can have it NOW if we will only line our lives up with the Word of God.

I commanded my skin to line up with His Word, which says "By His stripes I am healed" (I Peter 2:24). Anyone watching me would have thought I had gone off the deep end. With a loud voice, I commanded skin cancer to bow its' knee to the Name of Jesus.

> *I have sworn by Myself...that unto Me every knee shall bow, every tongue shall swear [allegiance].*
>   *ISAIAH 45:23*

> *That in the Name of Jesus every knee should (must) bow, in heaven and on earth and under the earth.*
>   *PHILIPPIANS 2:10*

> *...As I live, says the Lord, every knee shall bow to Me and every tongue shall confess to God.*
>   *ROMANS 14:11*

I decided, and decreed (loudly) that my skin cells, flesh, and body would now radiate the glory of God.

You shall also decide and decree a thing, and it shall be

*established for you; and the light (of God's favor)
shall shine upon your ways. JOB 22:28*

Then, I thanked God for it **before I ever saw any change;** praising Him for the victory! Though no visible changes were evident, and no improvements were seen, **I chose to look through the eyes of faith and victory,** and not through the eyes of fear, and defeat. Nothing could change what I believed, as I continued to speak only what the Word of God said. I knew the promise was mine, whether this side of heaven or the other, I was already healed; now my body needed to "line-up."

*...as I live says the Lord, what you have said in my
hearing I will do to you. NUMBERS 14:28*

HIS WORD WAS, AND IS, LIFE! I began to learn the power of words brought forth either life or death; the choice was mine according to the Bible.

*Death and life are in the power of the tongue and,
they who indulge in it shall eat the fruit of it
(whether for death or life). PROVERBS 18:21*

I learned quickly, that I no longer was under the curses listed in what the Bible calls the Book of the Law; curses I had inherited from the sinful lives of my ancestors, as well the sins I had myself committed.

*Deuteronomy Chapter 28
(excerpts)*

*But if you will not obey the voice of the Lord your
God, being watchful to do all His commandments and
His statutes which I command you this day, then all
these curses shall come upon you and overtake you; v. 15*

The Lord will make the pestilence cling to you; v. 21
The Lord will smite you with fever, consumption,
and inflammation... v. 22
The Lord will smite you with the boils of Egypt, and the
tumors, the scurvy, and the itch, from which you
cannot be healed... v. 27
with madness and dismay; v. 28

...oppressed, and robbed continually... v. 29
...you shall be driven mad by the sights which
your eyes shall see. v. 34

The Lord will smite you on the knees and on the legs
with a sore boil that cannot be healed, from the
sole of your foot to the top of your head. v. 35

You shall beget sons and daughters but shall not enjoy them,
for they shall go into captivity. v. 41

...then the Lord will bring upon you and your descendants
extraordinary strokes and blows, great plagues of long
continuance; grievous sickness of long duration. v. 59

Your life shall hang in doubt before you; day and night you
shall be very worried, and have no assurance of your life.
v. 66
In the morning you shall say,
Would that it were evening! And at evening you shall say,
Would that it were morning... because of the anxiety...
of your hearts... v. 67

These and many more curses come upon those who freely rebel against God's will for life; they had come upon me once, for this same reason. Now, I am covered with the redeeming Blood of Jesus Christ after having inherited the blessings found also in the Book of Deuteronomy Chapter 28.

If you will listen diligently to the voice of the Lord your God, being watchful to do His commandments which are commanded to you this day, the Lord your God will set you high above all the nations of the earth. v. 1

And all these blessings shall come upon you and overtake you if you heed the voice of the Lord... v. 2

Blessed shall you be in the city; blessed shall you be in the field. v. 3

Blessed shall be the fruit of your body... v. 4

Blessed shall be your basket... v. 5

Blessed shall you be when you come in (start) and blessed shall you be when you go out (end). v. 6

The Lord shall cause your enemies who rise up against you to be defeated before your face; they will come out against you one way and flee before you seven ways. v. 7

The Lord shall command the blessing upon you in your storehouse and in all that you undertake. And He will bless you in the land which the Lord your God gives you. v. 8

The Lord will establish you as a people holy to Himself, as He has sworn to you...if you walk in His ways... v. 9

And all people of the earth shall see that you are called by the name (and Presence) of the Lord, and they shall be afraid of you. v. 10

And the Lord shall make you have a surplus of prosperity,
through the fruit of your body, of your livestock,
and of your ground, in the land which the Lord
swore to your fathers to give to you.   v. 11
The Lord shall open to you His good treasury, the heavens,
to give the rain of your land in its season and to bless all the
work of your hands; and you shall lend to many nations,
but you shall not borrow.   v. 12

And the Lord shall make you the head and not the tail;
and you shall be above only, and you shall not be beneath,
if you heed the commandments of the Lord...   v.13

And you shall not turn aside from any of the words
which I command you this day,
to the right hand or to the left...   v.14

Daily, what came out of my mouth had to be what the Lord said in His Word, regardless of how I felt. *I had to agree with God* that I am blessed and cannot be cursed; above only and not beneath (my circumstances); the head and not the tail, in all things that attempt to divert or distract, depress or destroy me; and that I am healed of all sickness and disease by the wounding stripes that ripped open Jesus' back.

I must remain determined, *persisting to see myself as God sees me;* and not as I appear to be in my immediate surroundings, situations or circumstances. **I had to firmly believe** this *until I had the physical manifestation* of what it is I am needing; but the key here is to firmly believe without doubt whatsoever. *This is faith.* This is what breaks the yoke of destruction; a firm belief that what God has promised, He will also do, regardless of how I feel or what I see or even hear. Regardless of what the doctors report says,

God says I am healed; whether I feel healed or not does not change God's report.

He is the Final Authority, not man. His Word prevails, when mixed with faith; not man's word which is full of doubt and unbelief...even death. I have had more than my share of what this world has to offer, and all I can say is, *"No thanks."* It is a battle that takes place in the mind, will and emotions of us all. The enemy comes to taunt you, filling your mind with lies in an effort to get you to start speaking and believing, all that is contrary to God's Word. The enemy wants you to believe his lies over God's truth.

> *For the weapons of our warfare are not physical (weapons of flesh and blood), but they are mighty before God for the overthrow and destruction of strongholds (walls). (Inasmuch as we) refute arguments and theories and reasoning's and every proud and lofty thing that sets itself up against the (true) knowledge of God; and we lead every thought and purpose away captive into the obedience of Christ* II CORINTHIANS 10: 4, 5

The enemy (satan), will always insert ideas and thoughts that are not lined up with the Word of God. He inserts this in your mind, at your weakest moment; the only way in distinguishing between the enemy and the Holy Spirit is to be filled with the knowledge of God... *the Bible.*

It was during this battle to *retake all that satan had stolen from me,* that I was physically attacked by a male demon, known as an *incubus**. Keep in mind the door of opportunity that remained opened to the enemy, due to my continued living with my boyfriend, *now as a Christian!*

We were living in adultery, as well as fornication. Disobedience to what **I now knew** was sin, **gave legal entry** to the enemy, satan; *legal ground for him to not only enter, but operate in my life and home.*

As I lay in my bed *more asleep than awake,* I suddenly became aware of a dangerous presence in my room. I looked toward the bedroom door and saw what appeared to be a huge black body of vapor; almost as black as a cloud of exhaust fumes emitted from a bad muffler. This dark bodily form came closer toward me and an "alarm" went off inside me. I reached over to wake-up my (then) boyfriend. Before I could touch him, who was only inches away from me, I was instantly wrapped *or coiled* from the top of my head to my toes and audibly heard a swift wrapping of this serpent-like demon. I could hear the coiling of this thing, wrapping me!

The only thoughts racing through my mind were those of rape. The word "rape" kept repeating itself through my motionless, constricted, mind and body. I visibly saw this demon hovering just over me and physically was impressed upon by the weight of it lying against my body. I struggled to get up, realizing I was bound in place. I tried to scream, but could not, and I somehow knew if I could just **say** the Name of Jesus this demon would have to leave; *but I couldn't speak!* My tongue was gripped!

Panic fear tried to come over me as I quickly realized I couldn't move enough to waken my boyfriend, who was right next to me only inches away; I jerked repeatedly trying to free myself, trying to wake him, but the weight and grip of this demon overcame my own strength and will; as if paralyzing me.

I next recall a stirring in my own spirit, like a bubbling sensation, *rising up in me.* My spirit-man was calling on the Lord in a heavenly language; almost instantly the grip was broken over my tongue and body and I leaped out of my bed with the Name of Jesus freely flowing, gushing forth from my mouth... only to simultaneously incur the most incredible assault of violent burning sensation all over my body, all at once. Scratching and scraping, blood running down my legs, arms, neck, everywhere as my fingernails ripped open the newly formed skin layers, **I prayed.** Through tears, and Words of God aimed in warfare against this attack, I thanked God for healing me. I praised Him right in the face of this devil, that my healing was complete because of the shed Blood of Christ.

Not knowing why, I made it into the living room, rendering every weapon that was formed against me, helpless and without power, *in the name of Jesus,* (ISAIAH 54:17). Upon entering the front room, I saw what appeared to be a hazy, dark form... *not clear and surely not normal.* It was when I spoke the Blood of Jesus over my home in His name, that it completely left. I knew what it was, from my former life in practicing the evil of witchcraft.

Hours later, I realized everyone in the house had slept through it and was grateful, but confused. I questioned God as to why I had been attacked, being that now I was a Christian. All of this was new to me.

The Lord made it clear to me that **as a Christian,** a true Christian, *I could no longer live a compromising life.* I had to decide if I was going to live sinful or not, but *could not have it both ways.*

APRIL 1989

I had started to see the signs of healing on my skin; it was not until I separated myself from a compromising lifestyle, that I received a total and complete healing. Through a series of events, my boyfriend and I were removed from each other, and there was nothing we could do about it. God was in charge!

It was then that I began to understand what the Lord had been trying to show me, *how the sin of living with a man I was not married to hindered my complete healing from freely coming forth;* **how it affected everything.** Once the blocking obstacle of sin was removed, His healing power flowed toward and through me, as it was meant to... *without the hindrance of sin.*

One morning I woke up to find I was no longer stuck to my bed sheets. Upon a thorough examining of my body, I found my overall appearance to be free from every trace of fingernail scraped blood streaks and the skin was dried up! The color of my sore skin was now a faint pink, from a deep purple. All the pain of constantly scraping myself raw was now gone entirely and the welts that covered my entire body had now disappeared. For the first time in close to thirty months, I could shower completely emerged in water; *not a single cringe of pain. With the sin removed, I was healed and wholeness was emerging!*

Gradually, my hair stopped thinning out. I agreed with the Word of God that pertained to my hair in Matthew 10:30. I took the same authority over my hair, as silly as it sounds, as I had on my skin, and the results were the same! My hair began to come in, as full if not more, than it was before the skin disease. I was healed and restored from every physical ailment. I no longer had to shut myself in, behind double layered curtains. I could go in and out of any climate; the sun was no longer dreadfully painful to me as before. Fluorescent light didn't burn anymore. Carpet fibers didn't burn anymore! **I was healed!**

I was free, and remain free to this day. When symptoms

come, prayer and the continual agreement of God's Word in my life, deadens every symptom that forms against me.

What do you devise and plot against the Lord? <u>*He will make a full end; affliction shall not rise up the second time.*</u>
NAHUM 1:9

The Lord records His promise to put **an utter** (which means extreme, complete, unconditional, and overwhelming) end to this affliction (which means misery, and torment, anguish, curse, and plague), and it shall NOT arise again a second time. That is not to say that the *old symptoms will not try to return.* **But when they do,** we have a ***Blood-bought right*** to resist every single one of them, in the Power of His Name! We have God's own Word that those very symptoms are illegally trying to come upon us. They are trespassing! That promise, as all of them are, is also for you if you will ask Jesus to be the Lord of your life. Just invite Him in.

While searching for so many things in life, I saw more clearly how the Lord was even more than my Healer and Deliverer (or Liberator from evil). He was becoming my All, *in all.*

Fear not, for you shall not be ashamed; neither be confounded and depressed, for you shall not be put to shame. For you shall forget the shame of your youth... For your Maker is your Husband, the Lord of hosts is His name (ISAIAH 54:4)

Return, O faithless children, says the Lord, for I am Lord, Master and Husband to you, I will take you
JEREMIAH 3:14

And it shall be in that day, says the Lord, that you will call Me Husband...I will betroth you to Me forever; yes, I will betroth you to Me in righteousness and justice, steadfast

love and in mercy. I will even betroth you to Me in
stability and in faithfulness, and you shall know (intimately,
appreciate and cherish) the Lord.   HOSEA 2:16, 19, 20

Trusting the Lord *as my Husband,* I would depend on
Him for all my needs; *I had no job.*

Thus, says the Lord: Cursed (with great evil) is the strong
man who trusts in and relies on frail man, making weak
(human) flesh his arm (of strength), and whose mind and
heart turn aside from the Lord.   JEREMIAH 17:5

This warns us clearly of the dangers of bringing curses
upon ourselves, by relying and depending on people; *but I*
choose to be blessed...

(Most) blessed is the man who believes in, trusts in, and
who relies on the Lord, whose hope and confidence
the Lord is.   JEREMIAH 17:7

In trusting the Lord as my Husband, I now began to
depend on Him to remove all the shame I had learned to
accept. I was ashamed of myself in so many ways, for what
had happened to me so long ago. Sometimes I felt I could
have done more to protect myself. I punished myself for
not telling someone else what all had been happening to
me. Feeling so stained and believing that if anyone knew
the truth I would be hated, I kept silent and held the pain
within myself. I grew to believe that nice people did not
talk about such filthy things, and believed I would be
shunned if I tried to talk about such unspeakable pain.

I felt so bottled in, suffocating on the shame of my past,
with so many dirty secrets that no one wanted to hear; I did
not know anyone who could understand what I was feeling
or the depth of pain I was acquainted with. I believed with

all my heart that I was the only person who had ever experienced such agony, and I tried to guard my heart; *tried to protect the child that was still alive in me.* The child who had been stripped of trust and innocence. The same child who had cried alone in the dark, *for so long.*

If I say, surely the darkness shall cover me and the night shall be (the only) light about me, even the darkness hides nothing from You, but the night shines as the day...
PSALM 139:11, 12

"Through tears, and Words of God thrust through spiritual warfare against the enemy, I thanked God for healing me; I praised Him right in the face of this devil, that my healing was complete because of the shed Blood of Christ."

~ Sandra Cerda

CHAPTER SEVEN

JERICHO MUST FALL

July 1989

At about a month or so following the full manifestation of my physical healing I came to a place in my walk with my Lord where I could not advance. There were so many walls on my path that needed to come down.

I was so awed by the True and Living God that had entered my life, when I had begun to think there was no God. I would dig through His treasure chest of Words, seeking promises of gold, but this time I knew He wanted me to seek Him personally. His desire was for a more intimate, more personal acquaintance between me and Him, as the Restorer of Souls (Psalm 23:3 NKJV).

One afternoon, desperate to know why I sensed such a separation from God, desperate to know why it was as if my prayers were not being heard or answered, I fell on my knees and cried out to Him, "Show me what it is I'm not doing...what is it I haven't done; help me do it so I can come closer to you, Father." I cried out to Him for quite a while, and as I paused exhausted from all the crying out, I heard Him call my name; He said,

"Sandra, forgive"

Just as quickly as He said forgive, He revealed to my heart and mind the man who had physically assaulted me long ago as a child. There were others, but what needed to be pulled out was the root of all my bitterness; *and it was this man.* I could not forgive this man at all, in any way. He had stolen so much from me; I cried so hard before I finally said, *"Father, help me... help me forgive him. Help me want to forgive him. I don't know how to do this, Father."* My own strength was weak; my own will *was unwilling.* I knew it would take His strength working at this point in me, if I was ever going to be free to go on with my life.

He helped me. He helped me pray for this man's soul. He helped me release the fury and the vengeance I unknowingly held on to. He helped me release all the bitterness and hatred *I had denied was there,* for so long. Jesus Himself said when He hung on the cross at Calvary:

"Father, forgive them, for they know not what they do..."
LUKE 23:34

He said this after they spit on His face, tearing the beard right off His cheeks.

I gave My back to the smiters and My cheeks to those who plucked off the hair; I hid not My face from shame and spitting. ISAIAH 50:6

He said**, *"Father, forgive them",*** as they beat His head and face so severely He could not be recognized by the people who knew Him best. They took a whip tipped with sharp ends striking Him thirty-nine times, ripping His flesh wide open...He endured all this and more, and never opened His mouth against them. All this because He claimed to be the

Son of God. **He was Who He said He was.** He had done no wrong, was guilty of committing no sin, whatsoever; **He never lied.**

Hanging on the cross, pierced by His hands and feet, blood gushing from every area of His body, He cried out **"FATHER FORGIVE THEM; THEY KNOW NOT WHAT THEY DO".** When He was already dead, they pierced His side with a sword and He was emptied of every drop of blood...*for us.*

The Lord had helped me to see this **UNCONDITIONAL LOVE, UNCONDITIONAL FORGIVENESS** through His own eyes, for the man who had assaulted me as a child. It was then that I saw how this man was also a victim, a tool *used of satan.* My prayer for him became, *"Father, I forgive him, He never truly realized the pain he was causing; I ask You to forgive him also, Father."* This had to be a move of God, **for** *in the natural* <u>my mind, and my rationalizing of the circumstances</u> cried out for vengeance; cried, *"How could he not have known"?* Could it also be that he himself was a victim of incest, and he was bound as a slave to what he had been subject to as a child? only God knows; I believe the secret things belong to God.

I was not in a position where I could afford to make ridiculous excuses for his actions against me or *any child.* I had myself been a victim of incest, **and had not grown up to molest and violate other children!** My place was not to judge or condemn him, *but to love and forgive him...* to pray that the cords of bondage would be broken from his life. This was not possible at all in my own strength, ability, or will power, but in the strength that can only come from God, *of which I had to trust.*

*He (the Lord) will even deliver the one for whom you
intercede **who is not innocent;** yes, he will be delivered
through the cleanness of your hands.*   JOB 22:30

This verse of scripture records what God's promise is to me;
*and He was asking me to intercede in prayer for this man,
who was as guilty as sin!* He was asking me to do something
I knew was impossible for me to do. But He was willing to
help me. He was not asking me to do something He
Himself had not had to do thousands of years earlier. **He
too had known betrayal.**

The Lord helped me turn over all the feelings of betrayal
not only for the man who had bruised my soul, but for so
many others, *a little at a time.* God remains faithful to
forgive us when we ask Him to and we in turn must be
obediently willing to forgive those we remember have hurt us
in our past. **Evil says "hate", but love says "forgive".** He
knows every thought, secret purpose and intention that
cradles within our heart.

> *...He will bring to light the secret things that are
> (hidden) in darkness and disclose and expose
> the secret aims of hearts.*   II CORINTHIANS 4:5

If you are bound up in bitterness, pride or a sense of denial
in forgiving others, just ask Him to help. He is so willing to
free us from those ties that bind our soul. The curse that
followed my family, from generation to generation, was
broken when I asked Jesus Christ to set me free, forgive me
and wash me clean in His Blood and asked Him to fill me
with the power of God known as the Holy Spirit, spoken of
in Acts Chapter Two. I asked Him in tears, as I all too soon
realized that He truly was my only Hope.

And they were all filled with the Holy Spirit
and began to speak in other tongues (languages)
as the Spirit kept giving them clear loud expression
(in each tongue in appropriate words).   ACTS 2:4

The ties that bound my soul in anger were broken through forgiveness, and **only when I admitted what they were and faced them** in the strength and power of God, as only the Holy Spirit could do. You must keep in mind though, that it is a *process of healing* that continues gradually as you make progress in your walk with the Lord. There are so many people whose pain and bondage is the deep severe pain of sexual assault, as was my own; while it happens, that others may not have walked such dark paths in life, as well.

My emotions were bound through fear; I feared loss and rejection; betrayal and thoughts of unworthiness filled my mind. I lived in a constant sense of not being good enough, and believed I was not worthy to have true love and happiness. Bitterness set in, as did confusion.

My soul was shattered by incestuous assaults from a man I loved and trusted, *as well as others in my childhood.*

My will was beaten and bruised by the severely hard impositions of weak spirited men; *as a trail of pain was all that was left.*

Mentally my mind was many times, on the brink of shutting off, as the taunts of tormenting memories continued to haunt me in virtually every area of my life. But, I learned that nothing was too hard for the Lord.

Alas, Lord God! Behold, you have made the heavens and the earth by Your great power and by Your outstretched arm!   There is nothing too hard or wonderful for You.
JEREMIAH 32:17

I learned that He was not only able, but willing and ready to mend me by also replacing my stony heart with *a heart of flesh.*

> *A new heart will I give you and a new spirit will I put within you, and I will take away the stony heart out of your flesh and give you a heart of flesh. And I will put My Spirit within you...*
> EZEKIEL 36: 26, 27

When I gave myself to Him
just the way I was,
a mess without hope,
He became my only
Hope.

69

I, Paul, an apostle (special messenger) of Christ Jesus by appointment and by command of God our Savior and of **Christ Jesus, our Hope.** I TIMOTHY 1:1

I had tried to straighten out my own life so many times, but my own strength failed, my own power was useless. It was His Spirit that overcame me in love; just overshadowed me in His mercy, lifting me from the gutter; He empowered me with His own might.

He caused me to be able to stand and face the fiery darts of my past, boldly declaring, and "I AM FREE"! **He caused me to be able** to take my place in Him, equipped so when the enemy comes to crush me with guilt and condemn me with false and perverse accusations, I can declare out loud, "I AM REDEEMED BY THE BLOOD OF THE LAMB."

It was not easy to look back; often it would devastate me and bring me to great bouts of despair, but flowing toward me continually was His grace in a great and overflowing abundance that just carried me a little further at a time. I had *HIS strength enabling me* to overcome.

Though I formerly blasphemed and persecuted and was shamefully, and outrageously aggressively insulting (to Him), nevertheless I obtained mercy <u>because I had acted out of ignorance in sheer unbelief.</u> And the **grace of our Lord flowed out superabundantly and beyond measure for me.** *And was accompanied by faith and love that are to be realized in Jesus Christ.*
I TIMOTHY 1:13,14

With Him leading me by my right hand upholding me firmly with His love, *I was then able* to overcome satan. My past was no longer a torment, but a testimony... a testimony of healing... *the healing power of forgiveness*. It was not than I had to only forgive others, *but I had to forgive myself.* As I freed myself in His outpour of immeasurable comfort and love, I found that I was above the guilt and shame, and no longer crushed and overwhelmed beneath it.

I forgave myself for believing I was unworthy, and for all the wrong decisions made when I *"turned left, instead of right* in life as *He was leading me to do what was right.* **He helped free me *from myself.***

He made a Way in the cold wilderness of this lost world through the Lord Jesus Christ. He made crooked paths straight and rough places smooth, turned my darkness into light as He became the Light of my life.

One Christian woman, the lead Prayer Director in a mega-church and Station Manager of a Christian television station angrily came to me, and said, *"My testimony, my testimony...why don't you tell your testimony to the Lord and forget it."* But that's not what God's Word says! You need to know the Word of God *for yourself* and know God personally! Not giving myself the opportunity to know Him and His Word could have been fatal in my life, and can be for you. Not having a clear knowledge of the Word, will paralyze you against the attack of the enemy.

> *And they have overcome (conquered) him (satan)*
> *by the Blood of the Lamb and by the utterance of their*
> *testimony; for they did not love their own lives,*
> *even unto death.* REVELATION 12:11

It is the **continued testimony** of all Jesus Christ **has done, is doing, and will do** that empowers us against the lies and deceitful tactics of the enemy. God shows us how to be an overcomer through the power of our words. One way is testifying of Who Jesus Christ is, and how He has freed us from being slaves of sin and pain, anger and *even hate*. We may not immediately see the freedom operating in the natural physical realm of our lives, but our faith always calls forth what we see through our vision of hope.

> *And the Lord said, ... lift your eyes now and look*
> *from the place you are, northward, southward,*
> *eastward and westward; for all... you see I give to you*
> *and your descendants forever.* GENESIS 13: 14, 15

Get a vision of what you desire in your life, find the promises that pertain to your need and diligently confess it in the face of every contrary, adverse and hindering obstacle. Be determined to have all that is promised to you in the Word of God, no matter what anyone else thinks or says.

Testify the glory of His freedom revealed in us by the Holy Spirit. Come to know **Him** as the Father of mercy, comfort; your healer and provider... your husband, your everything. Let your testimony be a *demonstration of the deliverance* found in Jesus Christ, the Son of the Living God.

It is not enough to know the Bible, or quote scripture after scripture... it is knowing the Author of the Bible in a **personal** relationship that brings on the power of the Almighty. Have a desire to know the God of the universe, the God of all life, *the God of all that is.* Only because of what Jesus Christ did for us <u>can this be possible.</u>

> *For my **determined** purpose is that I may **know Him** (that*
> *I may **progressively become** more deeply and intimately*
> ***acquainted** with Him, perceiving and recognizing and*
> *understanding the wonders of His Person **more** strongly*
> *and **more** clearly), and that I may in that same way come to*

*know the power out-flowing from His resurrection (which it exerts over believers) and that I may share His sufferings as to be **continually** transformed (in the Spirit into His likeness even) to His death...*   PHILIPPIANS 3:10

Come to know Him; come to know God's love and allow yourself to be transformed continually into His image with the help and power of the Holy Spirit.

When you know who you are in Christ, you will be able to stand your ground at the voice and in the face of all adversity and opposing forces of evil, whether spiritual, emotional, or physical.

When you know who you are in Him, you will be able to defeat every contrary situation that attempts to steal from you, your family, and your life. There's only one way to do it, and that's to say yes to Jesus.

Evil says, "hate"
but love says, "forgive"

CHAPTER EIGHT

NEW CREATIONS

AUGUST 1989

What is impossible with me is possible with God.
LUKE 18:27

With God, all things are possible to those who believe and trust Him and will not doubt in their hearts. You say you are too far gone... His arm is not short that He cannot redeem you. Do you think you are too dirty from your past, like I once did? Allow God to remove the filthy rags of sin and guilt, washing you in His Precious Blood and dress you in garments of praise. He will only do what you ask Him to... only when you invite Him to do it. The God I serve will never impose on you, His own will. He gave you a freedom of choice all your own; freedom to choose life with Him, or death without Him.

I call heaven and earth to witness this day against you that I have set before you, life and death, the blessings and curses; choose life that you and your descendants may live... for He is your life and the length of your days.
DEUTERONOMY 30:19, 20

If you have ever blamed God for the life you have suffered, that's alright... so did I; then I learned who was at fault and really to blame. The one out to kill, steal from me, and utterly destroy all that I loved, was satan. The One who can and will forgive us, help us forgive ourselves and others, is the Father of mercy and no one else. Just ask Him, and He'll help you, too.

> *For I am persuaded beyond doubt, that neither death nor life, nor angels nor principalities, nor things impending and threatening nor things to come, nor powers, height nor depth, nor anything else in all creation will be able to separate us from the love of God which is in Christ Jesus our Lord.*   ROMANS 8:38, 39

We cannot really describe our pain, nor measure fear or courage, anger or the despair of betrayal... nor can ones' hope be measured. Beauty cannot be measured, nor happiness, or even progress, really. And I am persuaded beyond all doubt that nothing will **ever** be able to separate the love He has for us. It is so without the measures and limits of boundaries we find ourselves placing on literally everything we know.

> *Then you shall call, and the Lord will answer; You shall cry, and He will say, "Here I am." If you take away the yoke from your midst, the pointing of the finger, and speaking wickedness, if you extend your soul to the hungry and satisfy the afflicted soul, then your light shall dawn in the darkness, and your darkness shall be as the noonday. The Lord will guide you continually, and will satisfy your soul in drought, and strengthen your bones; You shall be like a watered garden, and like a spring of water, whose waters do not fail.*   ISAIAH 58:9-11

How often I found it very difficult to completely place my trust in God after so many years of betrayal and abandonment by others I had loved and trusted. He is near you as you struggle to turn to Him!

Multitudes, multitudes in the valley of decision! For the day of the Lord is near in the valley of decision.
JOEL 3:14 NKJV

Are you among the multitudes that yet have not made this life changing decision for the Lord Jesus Christ? He is so near you, warming your heart toward Himself. It is the Holy Spirit Who has placed this desire within you to even consider Jesus, or God. He is calling you to Himself; it is no accident, nor fate that thoughts of God, the Father, have entered your heart, for He is *wooing you,* drawing you to His Son Jesus. All you must do is respond by asking Him to enter your life. Trust that He is all He says He is and more; as you do this, your healing will begin, and as you continue you will be as a butterfly shedding its' cocoon, and spreading its' wings for the first time; no more in bondage, but free to spread your wings and fly.

Are you one who has made the forward decision to follow Jesus, and have become very comfortable in the place you are in right now? Maybe you feel your prayers have not been heard, or the Lord has withdrawn His presence from you. You have examined your life and found there is nothing dark or hidden, nor *unrepented* sin; still, the lines of communication just seem hindered and even down, for some reason.

He has promised never to leave you, never to forsake (abandon) you; the only reason it could be is that He has taken a step forward in your walk together through life, and is now calling you to a higher place, *and higher plateaus in your relationship with Him.*

*Draw **me, we** will run after You...*
SONG OF SOLOMON 1:4

As He draws you and you answer, His glory fills you full and overflowing, His presence surrounds you drawing others and giving them such a desire to run after Him, also.

> *Seek the Lord and His strength;* **yearn** *for and seek His face and to be in His presence* **continually***!*
> I CHRONICLES 16:11

It is the Glory of God to conceal a thing (like His presence), but the glory of kings (you, as a royal priesthood), is to search out a thing. **Search out His Presence.** Do not fall in the trap of searching out the healing or forgiveness, but seek **the One** Who heals, and forgives. *Seek God Himself;* discover that as you dwell in the richness of His presence all your needs will be met, the desires of your heart fulfilled. Forget yourself and all that concerns you in Him for **He** has promised to make it all perfect...be determined not to go opposite of Him. He alone will never fail you; *He is the Unfailing God.*

He will not line Himself up with the will of your own flesh, or carnal pleasures; **His** will always prevails and **His** will is always best.

> *Arise (from the depression and the prostration in which circumstances have kept you... rise up to a new life), shine (be radiant with the glory of the Lord), for your light has come and the glory of the Lord has risen upon you!* ISAIAH 60:1

Rise up from the heaviness that your past life has kept you bound to, and into a new life of freedom in Jesus Christ. Come to the place where you decide you are not willing to lose out on life *anymore.* Come to the place where you realize *who the real enemy is;* come to the place where you can truly say to yourself and to others, *"God is not to blame"!* When you can wake up in the morning and not dread another day of this life, or wish things were different all the time; when you can wake up in the morning and just praise God for another day... then you can honestly say you have peace in your life. Jesus Christ *is Peace.* Jesus Christ is the **Prince** of Peace.

He will fill you with Himself; love you and care for you like no one you have ever known, can. Have you ever wondered if you could just start all over...with Him you can! He washes away your stains completely, and will never remember them again. Yield to Him in pure obedience.

> *Call to Me, and I will answer you and show you*
> *great and mighty things fenced in and hidden,*
> *which you do not know (do not distinguish or recognize,*
> *have knowledge of nor understand).* JEREMIAH 33:3

It grieves Him to see you in such pain as He knows so well that the price has been paid to free you; how He longs to see you walk in your freedom. Calling you away, through the voice of His Holy Spirit, He encourages you to trust in Him; trust Him to remove the shame and all guilt of your past, and to heal the wounds of your soul that fester with infection...

> *Behold, I am doing a new thing!*
> *NOW it springs forth; do you not perceive and know it*
> *and will you not give heed to it?* ISAIAH 43:19

Although you may not *ever* forget what has happened to you as a child, or otherwise, the Lord will turn around what satan meant for evil and cause you to be able to progress in a healthy manner of life, *daily.* The memories will cease from taunting and tormenting your mind so you can know what it means to walk in the *"peace that surpasses all understanding"* found in Philippians 4:17; His peace will guard your mind and heart. But you must take the first step. You must make the first move toward God. You do this by demonstrating a desire in your heart for Him. You do this by going forward toward Him and all of what He stands for, shunning every opportunity the enemy will try to entice you with. You must turn away from temptations that you know are immoral or just plain wrong.

The enemy will always try to tempt you; that is his job, *so to speak.* Your job is to resist his temptations; *that's where the power lies.* That's where the blessings await you. Temptation is not sin; *it is only when you <u>give in to that temptation</u> and agree with it* by taking an active part in it, and becoming a willing participant of it, that you become a sinner. Yielding to temptation is sin, according to the Word of God. God makes a way of escape, when we stay in His perfect will!

HE IS RISEN

OH! The blessing the Lord has poured over me!
When He gave me His strength and victory.
With Him at my side...no one will I fear; I cry praises of
"GLORY" for the whole world to hear!
And who can tell me that I am a sinner? Forgiveness
through Christ made me a winner! My only regret is the time
that I lost...living for satan, my soul almost cost.
But...now a new creature in Christ am I;
purchased with His Blood, I've been glorified!
For only three days He died...Do you hear?
Christ Jesus is risen and within you, so near!
Praise be to God, for His glory has come! Our sins
are forgiven for He sent us His Son, who hung on the
cross and took them away, washed with His precious
Blood all in one day! Sing praises to the Living God,
Glory! Hallelujah!
Christ Jesus is the Living God! He is the Messiah!
Cry praises of glory for the whole world to hear;
Christ Jesus is risen and within you, so near!

CHAPTER NINE

ARMED FOR BATTLE

$\mathcal{F}$rom the very first day I received Jesus Christ as my Lord, I discovered the value of Spiritual Warfare. When I realized the unsurpassing power of the Word of God, I armed myself daily with what He calls the Sword of the Spirit. With this Sword *(Word of God)*, I can stand my ground firmly against the onslaught of the enemy. But it takes more than just a sword for any warrior to enter the battle arena. In Ephesians Chapter Six, God has outlined the armor of the spirit needed for spiritual war, that we should place over our lives daily with our words, or by the confession of His Word.

> *In conclusion, be strong in the Lord (empowered*
> *through your union with Him); draw your strength from*
> *Him;* ***PUT ON*** *God's* ***WHOLE*** *Armor...* ***that you***
> ***may be able to stand up against*** *(all) the strategies*
> *and the deceits of the devil. For we are not wrestling with*
> *flesh and blood (only with physical opponents) ... but against*
> *the powers, against (master spirits who are) ...world rulers*
> *of this present darkness, against the spirit forces of*
> *wickedness in the heavenly (supernatural) sphere.*
> *Therefore,* ***PUT ON*** *God's complete armor,* ***that you***
> ***may be able to resist and stand*** *your ground on the*
> *evil day (of danger), and, having done all (the crisis)*
> *demands) ...stand (firmly in your place). Stand therefore*
> *(hold your ground), having tightened the belt of truth*
> *around your loins, having put on the breastplate of*
> *integrity and ...right standing with God ... having shod in*
> *preparation (to face the enemy with the firm-footed*
> *promptness and readiness that is produced by) of the*

Gospel of Peace. Lift up over all the (covering) shield of saving faith, upon which you can quench all the flaming missiles of the wicked (one). And take the helmet of salvation and the **sword that the Spirit wields (meaning puts into action),** *which is the Word of God. Pray at all times (on every occasion) in the spirit, with all prayer and entreaty.* **To that end keep alert and watch with strong purpose and perseverance,** *interceding in behalf of all the saints (God's consecrated people).* EPHESIANS 6:10-18

You enter the spirit realm of combat against spirit forces that come to steal, kill and destroy all that is precious to you, and to God. These spirit forces of darkness and evil have no respect for financial status or heritage, age, color or nationality ...I know of only One name that will render and produce this pure wickedness helpless, it is the Name of the Lord Jesus Christ.

Therefore (because He stooped so low) God has highly exalted Him and has freely bestowed on Him the name that is above every name, that in the Name of Jesus every knee must bow, in heaven and on earth and under the earth, and every tongue confess that Jesus Christ is Lord, to the glory of God, the Father. PHILIPPIANS 2:9-11

Not just anyone can enter the battle arena with the Name of Jesus. Accepting the Lord Jesus and renouncing the satanic hold over your life will give you the authority to obtain the (spiritually) legal use of His Name. Power is demonstrated as legal use of His Name is exercised.

In Acts Chapter 19, we learn how the need for this legal authority, along with a personal union with Christ is so great.

*Then some of the traveling Jewish exorcists {men who
adjure (charge, bind, or command by authority) evil
spirits} also undertook to call the name of the Lord Jesus
over those who had evil spirits, saying, I solemnly implore
and charge you by the Jesus Whom (the apostle) Paul
preaches! ... but (one) evil spirit replied, Jesus I know,
and Paul I know about, but who are you?* ACTS 19:14-15

The demons know Jesus, and when you become a child of
God they will also know you bear His name and authority
over them as you exercise His Name against them.

*Then the man in whom the evil spirit dwelt leaped
upon them, mastering two of them, and was so violent
against them that they dashed out of that house (in fear),
stripped naked and wounded. Many also of those
who were now believers came making full confession
and thoroughly exposing their
(former deceptive and evil) practices.* ACTS 19:16-18

Whether you are already a believer in Christ Jesus or not,
nothing is ever hidden from God. We are only deceiving
ourselves when we think for a moment we have kept
something from Him. He created the eyes to see and the
ears to hear, and nothing escapes Him; nothing will ever be
hidden from Him that will not be revealed in His good time.

*...for He will both bring to light the secret things that
are [now hidden] in darkness and disclose and expose the
[secret] aims of hearts. Then every man will receive his
[due] commendation from God.* I CORINTHIANS 4:5

You must know Him personally, and to do that takes but a
sincere desire of the heart.

*Delight yourself also in the Lord, and He will give you
the desires and secret petitions of your heart.*
PSALM 37:4

It's not the preacher's knowledge of Him that will save,
deliver and heal you. You must go a step further than
ministers of the Gospel, and seek Him out for yourself. It
was not the preacher's faith in God that healed me; I
stretched my faith out toward God, and took hold of His
garments, letting go for nothing and no one. My reach far
exceeded my grasp as I aimed for the very throne room of
the Almighty.

*I had gone but a little way past them [ministers] when
I found Him Whom my soul loves. I held Him and
would not let Him go...* SONG OF SOLOMON 3:4

So many people look to the preacher as if he were God, with
no faults, when it is Jesus alone Who is without fault. All
men of God are as human as any of us, and liable to fall
short in many areas of life. If we can keep our eyes off the
preacher and on the Lord alone, we will save ourselves a lot
of disappointments.

It was not my aunt's faith that set me free, delivering me
from all binding strongholds, that Saturday night in 1989.
Neither was it Pastor Osteen or Dodies' faith that healed me
when they prayed; it was my faith that reached out to God
and took hold of the Truth of His Word. My faith in God's
ability and unfailing promise healed me and made me
whole.

A woman who had suffered from a flow of blood for twelve
years, spending all her living on physicians, could not be
healed by anyone, came up behind Him and touched the
fringe of His garment; immediately her flow of blood ceased.

*And Jesus said, who is it who touched Me? ...some-
one did touch Me; for I perceived that [healing] power
has gone forth from Me. And the woman ...declared in
the presence of all the people for what reason she had
touched Him and how she had been instantly cured. And
He said to her, Daughter, **your faith** (your confidence
and trust in Me) **has made you well!** Go in peace.*
LUKE 8:43-38

Reach out to God; *allow your faith in His ability,* to reach Him and heal you in every area of your spirit, soul and body, so that you may also go forward in peace.

My relationship with the Lord intensified and became stronger after I became aware of His understanding me; comforting me with His love drew me into a deeper, more secure trust in God.

TODATE...

I am no longer torn apart when I recall the past. I no longer feel cheated. I would say that even now when I reflect on what once happened, *and what might have been,* I no longer see myself as the victim. Because of a true revealing of who Christ is, *I am whole now.* Not someone's twisted interpretation of Christ's person; but a *soul-restoring experience,* first hand... that is equally available to *anyone* who wants it.

If you need healing in your life, if you need a Savior, a Redeemer, and if you need the Restorer of souls *to center your soul,* entering your life, and filling you with the glory of His Holy Spirit, and if you need a new chance at life... A **LIFE THAT IS ALIVE WITH LIFE,** then please pray this prayer out loud:

> *Dear Jesus, help me. There is much pain in my heart, heal me now, Lord. Come into my life and change me; be my Lord. I ask You to make me the person You always intended me to be. Open my eyes to Your Truth. Forgive those who have scarred me and help me to forgive them also, in Your strength. Make me understand the Word of Your instruction. Restore my soul; make me whole. Raise me up and strengthen me; cleanse me and renew a right spirit in me and remove from me the way of falsehood, and unfaithfulness to You. Fill me with Your Holy Spirit, for I have chosen this way of Truth, Life and Faithfulness. Holy Spirit, teach me how to love and be loved...help me walk in the Light of my God. I give my life to You, Lord Jesus, asking You to give me a heart that is willing to fulfill the call You have on my life. Conform me and mold me to Your perfect will, Father. I love You, Jesus. Thank You for all that You have done. Help me see through Your eyes all the days of this life, and turn my eyes from beholding vanity, idols and idolatry; restore*

*me to vigorous life and health. Give me renewed life, in
the Name of Jesus, I pray. Amen.*

Once you have prayed this prayer, I encourage you to call
and share this with someone. Let us rejoice at the new-
found freedom in Christ, that you have entered. At the end
of this book are some numbers you can call. Caring people
are on the other line, waiting.

Now, addressing satan with the whole authority of the Holy
Spirit in you and in the Name of Jesus... say out loud:

*Satan, I renounce your hold from my life, in the Name of
Jesus Christ Whom I serve. I'll serve you no more satan,
nor will I serve or surrender to the wayward direction of this
world, in Jesus' Name. Loose your hold on all my blessings,
and return all you've stole from me, according to the Word,
that says in Proverbs 6:30,31, "When the thief has been found
out, he must restore seven times (what he stole) ..." and you
satan have been found out. Now I command you to restore
seven times what I know you have stolen, in Jesus Name.*

Now that you are a child of God, and your blessings are on
their way according to His Word, begin to praise Him.
Begin confessing that you receive them, before any evidence
is seen. See His promise of overflowing abundance through
the eyes of faith, and take your eyes off all that surrounds
you.

The Lord provides His angels for your assistance.

*Are not the angels all ministering spirits (servants)
sent out in the service (of God for the assistance) of
those who are to inherit salvation?* HEBREWS 1:14

By having the authority to activate the Name of Jesus, you may ask the angels God has assigned to you to go forth, in His Name and stir up your blessings, and to deliver them to your life! Whatever you need assistance in, *ask in Jesus Name* and receive all that is lined up in the Word of God.

Enter a new realm of life. Come now into the reality of what life should be, and not what this world has misled you to believe. For so long we have been fed lies, and half-truths; the time has come now to shake off the dust of this worlds' deception and to rise and go forward in victory.

We no longer must allow the slavery of agonizing that sexual assault breeds, to keep us captive. Know the Truth of Who God really is and of how much He loves you, and be set free from the weight of shame and guilt you have carried for so long. Unforgiveness is heavy; Ask Him to take the load, *and He will;* He will heal all that you ask, restore everything to its original intended order, and refresh you with Himself, when you ask Him with all your heart.

Walls cannot hinder My glory; no,
the power of My glory will manifest. I will show Myself
wherever My children are and the whole world will see
My glory radiating through them, says the Lord...

PROPHECY 1989 - JOHN OSTEEN

My prayer for you, is this:

May the perfect peace of God guard your heart and mind as you process through to your healing. That you would find yourself complete in Him, and enter a liberty that is found only in His healing touch. That you will have joy, and find healing, through forgiveness!

May the Lord bless you and keep you;
May He make His face shine upon you;
May He lift His countenance upon you
and give you peace.

Love,
Sandra

My beloved speaks and says to me,
Rise up, my love, my fair one,
and come away.
For behold, the winter is past;
the rain is over and gone...

SONG OF SOLOMON 2:10,11

CHAPTER TEN

SEXUAL ABUSE:
EFFECTS ON THE VICTIM
Information submitted by:
Certified Christian Counselor: Tamara Johnson-Macleod, Houston, TX.

A female, child-victim, of sexual assault, sexual abuse or incest tends to appear quite precocious, or mature. This is because her role (in the family) has been sexualized and because she has been forced into the role of wife in the home/family. Many women molested as children, claim that they were robbed of their childhood, feeling that their early needs for appropriate nurturing were not met. Because their emotional development has been arrested, child victims often demonstrate a pseudo-maturity (a false maturity), that masks their need for normal parental affection.

Feeling responsible for what has happened and resulting guilt over it appear to be somewhat intensified in victims of sexual assault, in this case incest. One reason for intensified guilt relates to the complex intra-familial dynamics, or complex mental and spiritual energy within the family unit, and to the fact that these youngsters already have had relationships with offenders prior to the onset of sexual assault. They reason that they *"could have done something"* to prevent the sexual assault/incest or stop the abuse once it started.

Guilt also is compounded by the fact that most victims do not disclose sexual abuse, sexual assault or incest when it first starts. When they do tell someone, their guilt is exacerbated because of the ramifications of disclosure. In cases of incest, will the relative go to jail? What about the family income? Will the family dissolve?

Victims feel responsible for incest, for example, partly because, unconsciously or consciously, they know it is wrong. They wonder, *"why me"?* Why is my relative doing this to me? Some victims wonder why *they* were chosen instead of another child in the family. These feelings intensify alienation from family and peers and a sense of being somehow *"different"*. This gives room for a sense of rejection and confusion.

Victims' **loss of trust** in authority figures is one of the most devastating effects of incest. Parents and close family members are the first adult's children learn to trust, and incest represents **ultimate betrayal** of that trust. Hence, victims tend to be suspicious of authority figures and, in therapy, are slow to open up and reveal their true feelings. It is quite common for victims first to tell their peers about the occurrence of incest in the family. Having learned to be wary of adults, they tend to fear confiding in them and may also doubt that an adult will believe what they say.

These issues related to trust, responsibility, intimacy, thwarted needs for nurturance and *blocked affect (mood),* have long-term implications for incest victims, who later experience a variety of problems as they seek mature adult relationships. It is especially difficult for victims to trust males or to establish deep and intimate interpersonal relationships. In addition, women whose early needs were neglected lack basic skills and lack parenting their own young. Due to complex feelings resulting from incestuous abuse, victims experience a high level of/or **repressed rage.** Consequently, anger is turned inward as victims become involved in a variety of self-destructive behaviors including suicide threats and attempts, self-mutilation, chemical abuse and prostitution. When married, some victims set the stage for molestation of their daughters either to relive vicariously their own unresolved trauma, to avoid intimacy with their spouses, or as an expression of displaced anger. Victims not only feel anger toward their attacker, but also toward other family members, and toward themselves for submitting to their attacker.

Summary of Common Short/Long-Term Effects of Childhood Sexual Assault

SHORT-TERM PHYSICAL
Urogenital/anal injuries and irritation
Presence of semen (vaginal, rectal, oral)
V.D. (oral, rectal, urogenital)
Anal enlargement
Pregnancy
Psychosomatic symptoms

LONG TERM PHYSICAL
Homophobia
Homosexuality
Time-bomb effect/Post-Traumatic Stress Reaction
Problems with parenting
Sexual dysfunction
Relationship problems (trust/intimacy)
Splitting/dissociative and conversion states
Multiple personality
Psychosis
Child molestation (victimizing others)

BEHAVIORIAL
Affective problems (depression, fears/phobias, guilt,
anger, low self-esteem, self-blame, alienation,
detachment, emotional disconnection)
Social withdrawal
Suicidal tendencies or suicide attempts
Psychosomatic manifestations
Chemical abuse (alcohol and drugs)

Lack of autonomy (self-control)
    Lying and manipulation
    Sleep disorders (nightmares)
    Self-mutilation
    Sexual promiscuity or aversion to sex
    Seductive behavior
    Use of precocious sexual language
    Delinquent acting out behavior
    School truancy
    Cruelty to animals
    Functional enuresis/encopresis (bed-wetting)
    Runaway behavior
    Fear of/aversion to sports
    Regression (thumb-sucking, baby talk)
    Autoerotic preoccupation (excessive masturbation)

ABOUT THE AUTHOR

Sandra was ordained through the laying on of hands, by the late John Osteen of Lakewood Church, Houston, TX., in 1991. She has appeared on the 700 Club and HEART TO HEART with contemporary Christian Music Artist and Author, Sheila Walsh, Daystar's Taking a Break with Joni Lamb and more.

Her ministry of *"healing through forgiveness"* exposes the snare of bitterness brought forth through sexual assault as a child, sexual assault as a teen, domestic violence, drug and alcohol addiction and suicide as well as the occult... all of which the power of God has freed her from. Her story of God's *healing and delivering power* has continued to inspire people around the world.

Sandra is the Founding Pastor of New Life Ministries, serving as Pastor and Director of Ministries. She is the pioneer for the *Gathering of Warriors Crusades,* in Texas, and **Emerge**, *a Ministry to the Broken.* Sandra is currently working on her first novel/film on the life of Mary Magdalene. For more on The Magdalene Project, visit www.MaryMagdalene.Film

She resides in the suburbs of Houston, Tx., with her large and growing family and her warrior husband of 30 years!.

ABOUT THE MINISTRY

Sandra Cerda is Director of Emerge: A Ministry to the Broken, and freely shares her story wherever she is asked. She serves through public speaking, addressing the issues of sexual indecency in it's every form; she also serves through her writing. Sandra is the Visionary and Executive Producer of Magdalene: *For Life & Love*, a book/film project. For more, please visit **www.MaryMagdalene.Film**

NEW LIFE MINISTRIES, reaches out to hurting people trapped by the shadows of their past. Crusades, such as the *Gathering of Warriors,* continue to blaze throughout the region where a powerful demonstration of the Holy Spirit fills the atmosphere and whereby lives are dramatically changed. Through the Prophetic Spiritual Warfare mantle on this ministry people are set free, *to the glory of God.*

Internationally, financial and practical support to pastors and churches in Chile, Germany, Pakistan, Croatia, Hungary, Mexico, India, Egypt, Viet Nam, Bulgaria and many, many more, having gleaned the urgency for International Missions Support through their Pastors and Spiritual Parents, John and Dodie Osteen.

NEW LIFE MINISTRIES can be caught on YouTube, at
www.youtube.com/SandraCerda

Her Books are available around the world on Amazon @
Amazon/Books/Sandra Cerda

My sincere appreciation to all who have labored in love, for the completion of this project. Without whose help, I know I could not have accomplished this. All the seeds you have planted in doing what you have will bring back a harvest into your lives and freedom to the lives of many:

John and Dodie Osteen. Their prayers and constant encouragement held my arms up in the face of many battles.

My love and appreciation to the New Life Ministry team, and most especially to my mother for all her prayers, inspiration and instruction; I am grateful.

My greatest appreciation goes to the Lord for healing my life.

OTHER BOOKS BY SANDRA CERDA
on Amazon.com and Barnes & Noble

Magdalene: *For Life & Love*
(available at www.MaryMagdalene.Film)

Water Me, Lord! (Women's Devotional) © 2011, 2017

DREAM PEACE: When God Speaks
A Scriptural Journey on Dream Interpretation © 2011, 2017

SPIRITUAL WARFARE
The Fight, The Freedom, The Fire ©2011, 2017

Get Connected, here:
www.cerdaministries.org

YouTube/alandsandracerda
Blog: sandracerda@blogspot.com
Twitter@alandsandra
Facebook.com/cerdaministries
www.google.com/SandraCerdaAuthor
Google+/alandsandracerda

If you or your loved one is suffering the victimization of
incest, *there is help.* Contact:

THE INCEST HOTLINE
1-800-4A-CHILD

New Life Ministries
www.cerdaministries.org

New Life Publishing

Bringing **1st Time Authors**, to *print!*

On Facebook@1stTimeAuthors